THE
DALAI
LAMA

THE DALAI LAMA

LEADERSHIP AND THE POWER OF COMPASSION

Text and photography by
Ginger Chih *(Tenzin Yangchen)*

Foreword by
His Holiness the Fourteenth Dalai Lama

Interlink Books

An imprint of Interlink Publishing Group, Inc.

Northampton, Massachusetts

In Collaboration with The Tibet Fund

First paperback edition published in 2024 by
Interlink Books
An imprint of Interlink Publishing Group, Inc.
46 Crosby Street, Northampton, Massachusetts 01060
www.interlinkbooks.com

Library of Congress Cataloging-in-Publication Data available
ISBN-13: 978-1-62371-704-9 (paperback)

Publisher: Michel Moushabeck
Editor: Jane Bugaeva
Cover design and interior design: Harrison Williams
Production: Pam Fontes-May
Proofreading: Jennifer McKenna

Printed and bound in Korea
10 9 8 7 6 5 4 3 2 1

CONTENTS

PREFACE   7
FOREWORD   9
INTRODUCTION   11

THE AUTHOR'S STORY   17

THE DALAI LAMA'S STORY: ESCAPE   19
THE DALAI LAMA'S STORY: LEADER OF THE TIBETANS   29
Educating the Future   35
   Reestablishing the Tibetan Government in Exile   47
   Creating the Capital   51
   Rebuilding Communities   63
   In Search of Nomads   77
   A Decade Later   91
   Self-Supporting People   95
   Tibetans in the West   103
   Modernizing Tibetan Culture   111

THE DALAI LAMA'S STORY: SPIRITUAL LEADER   115
Preserving Tibetan Buddhist Culture   121
   Preserving Ancient Traditions   131
   Reestablishing Monasteries   137
   Compassion at Work   143
   Promoting Nuns' Education   145
   Ordination Ceremonies   153
   Old and New Buddhists   157
Vision for a Better World: Spiritual and Ethical Revolution   165
   The Power of Compassion and Love   166
   Cultivating Lasting Happiness and Inner Peace   167
   Universal Responsibility   170
   Embracing Everyone as His Family   170

THE DALAI LAMA'S STORY: A GLOBAL LEADER   173

    Developing Global Responsibility   177

    Scientist of the Heart and Mind   183

    The 33rd Mind and Life Dialogue   193

    Pragmatic Leader   195

    Visionary Leader   197

    Ethical Leader   199

       Educating Future Generations   199

       Our Natural Environment   202

       Interreligious Harmony   203

       Peace and Disarmament   205

    Vision for Tibet: Zone of Peace   207

CONCLUSION   211

BIBLIOGRAPHY   216

ACKNOWLEDGMENTS   217

PEOPLE INTERVIEWED AND CONSULTED   218

PLACES VISITED   221

ENDNOTES   224

PREFACE

In 1995, the Tibetan Community in exile was chosen as one of the 50 exemplary communities for "We the Peoples: 50 Communities Awards," presented while commemorating the 50th anniversary of the founding of the United Nations on October 24, 1995. This award meant a lot for many of us who have spent the best part of our lives serving fellow Tibetans in exile. I feel fortunate to have been a part of envisioning and implanting the Tibet Fund's mission, from my 16 years of service in Nepal and 31 years with the Office of Tibet and the Tibet Fund in the United States.

In 2009, I met Dr. Ginger Chih, who kindly volunteered to photograph the Tibetan community in exile, predominantly in India and Nepal, on behalf of the Tibet Fund. Then in 2018, she met His Holiness the Dalai Lama who gave her unprecedented access. It has been a pleasure collaborating with Dr. Chih for this illustrated book. Due to her multicultural background, Dr. Chih is highly sympathetic towards the plight of the Tibetan refugees. As a Buddhist, she adopts the teachings of His Holiness the Dalai Lama into her daily life and professional work. As a beneficiary of Tibetan Buddhist teachings and its meditative practices, she has decided to bring to bear her skills as a documentary photographer to highlight the situation of the Tibetan diaspora and the challenges Tibetans are facing as they struggle to preserve their unique cultural and national identity in exile.

Dr. Chih has meticulously documented numerous visits to Tibetan refugee communities in India, Nepal, Europe, and North America as a way of expressing her appreciation to the Tibetan community. Dr. Chih wanted to document the plight of the Tibetan diaspora as community members struggled to maintain and preserve their unique and rich religious, cultural, and spiritual identities and traditions. For this project, Dr. Chih has taken photographs showcasing various aspects of the Tibetan community, from life in the settlements to education, religion, and culture.

Dr. Chih vividly tells the story of H.H. the Dalai Lama's escape to India, reestablishing the Tibetan Government in Exile and the establishment of Tibetan refugee communities around the globe. As the age-old saying goes, a picture is worth a thousand words, and Dr. Chih's images communicate the condition of the Tibetan diaspora with immediacy and accuracy. Anyone who sees these photographs will experience the sights and sounds of Tibetan life in exile as if they were there themselves.

Rinchen Dharlo, President Emeritus, THE TIBET FUND

Bronze statue of Chenrezig (Tibetan) or Avalokitsvara (Sanskrit), who embodies compassion. Library of Tibetan Works and Archives

THE DALAI LAMA

FOREWORD

A few years back, Ms. Ginger Chih came to see me in Dharamsala during which she showed me photographs that she had taken of Tibetan communities in India and Nepal over the course of a decade. Her intimate portraits and narrative demonstrates the resilience and strength of the Tibetan people.

We first reached India as refugees in 1959 after the failure of our sincere efforts for nine years at peaceful coexistence with the communist Chinese authorities who took over Tibet. At that time, as we Tibetans say, 'all we knew was the ground below and the sky above.' Today, the Tibetan people in exile have been able to make a mark in the world.

This illustrated book provides an insight into Tibetan Buddhist culture, a culture of peace and compassion. It reveals how Tibetans in the diaspora have, in the face of great adversity, managed to protect and preserve our distinct cultural heritage. The principles of non-violence and compassion that lie at the heart of our culture have the potential to make an important contribution to peace and harmony throughout world.

14 January 2021

Photo of Dr. Ginger Chih with His Holiness the Fourteenth Dalai Lama by Tenzin Choejar

INTRODUCTION

I first saw the Dalai Lama in Zurich in 2005 where he conducted a public teaching for an audience of 10,000 people. When he entered, the stadium filled with positive energy and excitement. We were all captivated by his charismatic presence and message of compassion. He spoke to the critical issues of our world—injustice, suffering, poverty, and materialism. He was passionate about how humans abuse our only home, the planet earth. He told us we could each make a difference by taking small steps. I believed him and could see others did, too. We left the stadium with glowing faces, each of us contemplating what action we personally could take to make a difference in the world. I began to study Tibetan Buddhism and to travel to attend the Dalai Lama's Buddhist and public teachings.

While the Dalai Lama ignited my interest in Tibetan Buddhism, I soon became fascinated with the people themselves. How did my travels to document Tibetan culture and people begin? Serendipity? Luck? My journey started from a chance encounter on a railroad platform in Hyderabad, India, after attending a thirteen-day teaching given by the Dalai Lama in 2006. Getting back to London, where I lived, involved riding an overnight train to Hyderabad, spending the night there and boarding a flight to London. Although we had booked a hotel for the night, ours was canceled. As we were considering what to do, an American woman offered her hotel room for the night as she was heading to Africa that evening and only needed to rest during the day. Through her, I heard about the Tibet Fund, a non-profit organization that provides cultural support and development programs to the Tibetan refugees living in India and Nepal. My passion started by serendipitously hearing from an acquaintance that the Tibet Fund wanted to make a photographic documentation of the world-wide Tibetan diaspora. This project appealed to me since I had worked as a documentary photographer for nearly ten years and was a student of Tibetan Buddhist teachings and its meditative practices. I had integrated Tibetan Buddhist philosophy into my work as a management consultant and executive coach for international multicultural businesses. I felt it was time for me to give something back to the Tibetan people, so I volunteered.

When I began my travels related to the project in 2009, I had no knowledge of the scope of the diaspora. I traveled alone to all the twenty-four major Tibetan settlements in India and Nepal, as well as to other cities and towns in India, Nepal, Europe, and North America, where a large number of exiled Tibetans live. I stayed in all kinds of accommodations, including settlement guest quarters, guesthouses operated by Tibetans, a monastery, private homes, and even in a nomad tent. I shared the refugees' everyday lives, including food and even some power outages. But more so, I was captivated and deeply moved by the warmth and calm strength of the Tibetans in exile, as demonstrated in the many events I witnessed and stories told to me. Above all, I have been inspired by the Tibetan people's unwavering dedication to maintaining their cultural and spiritual traditions. Although my journey had a fortuitous beginning, first from hearing the inspiring words of the Dalai Lama, then from a compassionate stranger in a crowded train station, it soon developed real purpose. I feel compelled to tell the story of the Tibetan diaspora because of a parallel to my own refugee journey; I am also displaced from my homeland.

Who am I? I am a traveler and an explorer of cultures. I have lived in many places where I didn't feel I belonged. I have visited even more places where I knew I was an outsider. Although I was by no means a part of any of the Tibetan settlements, I also didn't feel I was a total stranger. Instead of hostility since I am part Chinese, they thanked me for doing this project—especially *because* I am part Chinese. I mentioned this to a Tibetan who said, "It's because the Dalai Lama has been telling us not to hate the Chinese people. He has taught us to distinguish between the people and the government." He added, "Had you been traveling among us during the early refugee years, you would have had a very different experience." Subsequently, I have heard other Tibetans share what the Dalai Lama taught them. It was obvious how much respect and love they feel towards him.

The Tibetan diaspora is a group of Tibetans in exile. Their lives and stories are filled with upheavals and continual transitions. My journey into the communities of Tibet would not have been possible without the guidance and insight from many along the way. One such person is Dorje Gyaltsen, a refugee as an infant and orphaned at a very young age when first his mother, then his father, died working on road construction. He said he owed everything to the Tibetan Children's Village (TCV): the school gave him a home, cared for him as an orphan, and then educated him. He met his wife, also an orphan, at TCV. I asked Dorje how they could maintain such calm strength in the face of such tragedy. He told me that everyone was in the same situation, so there was no sense in feeling sorry for himself. Furthermore, he added, if the people didn't work together to create a new future, no one would have survived! Very quickly, Dorjee became my friend and teacher of Tibetan culture. Dorje took me to see people who were not on the itinerary—especially since he knew I was studying Tibetan Buddhism. I soon learned first-hand what remarkable experiences can take place when one is present and accepts what a random meeting can lead to—the gifts the universe presents.

The Dalai Lama is the Tibetan people's treasured leader; he serves as a leader to Tibetans in Tibet and the worldwide diaspora, thus uniting them in their aspiration for a free Tibet. The Dalai Lama has defined and exemplified Tibetan culture in a modern world, making it relevant. He has shown the Tibetans that the value of their culture is inseparable from their spiritual tradition. In doing so, he has given the Tibetans a sense of pride and a compelling reason for preserving their culture.

The narrative of the Tibetan diaspora, a community of 150,000 people, is intertwined and inseparable from Buddhism and their spiritual leader. Always seeing the positive side of any situation, the Dalai Lama has reiterated that the exile situation has provided opportunities for change. He developed a very clear vision of what had to be done and provided the guiding principles on how to do it. He guided the exiled Tibetans from an insulated existence into a complex and interconnected world. Theirs had been a hierarchical society ingrained to defer to authority figures. The Dalai Lama had wanted to modify the system of governance even before his exile. In exile, he initiated the process of democratization. The Tibetan success story is largely due to the vision and guiding principles set out by the Dalai Lama, who saw the modernization of Tibetan society and democracy as essential elements of preservation and growth. He is a role model of how a Tibetan can actively participate and contribute to the global world. Believing that Tibetan culture can only survive when it is modernized, the Dalai Lama has adopted the principles of democracy, non-violence, and human rights, interpreted them within Buddhism, and applied them to Tibetan culture and politics. The Dalai Lama has led the Tibetan freedom struggle on a path of non-violence and has consistently sought a mutually agreeable solution in the spirit of reconciliation and compromise with the Chinese government. He was awarded the Nobel Peace Prize in 1989 for his unwavering insistence on non-violence to achieve freedom.

Over the course of my travels, I have seen how the Dalai Lama's vision has transformed every aspect of Tibetan society—from local government, education, women's rights, and monastic practices to the study and practice of Buddhism by lay people. Tibetan traditions now accommodate and reflect the modern world, thus enabling Tibetan culture to remain relevant, vibrant, and purposeful. I was therefore especially eager to meet with the Dalai Lama in person—to understand how a person who grew up so secluded and educated in ancient tradition could become a transformative leader among the Tibetan diasporas. I assumed that, like hundreds of others, I would be observing him from afar. Karma intervened! Most mornings when the Dalai Lama is not traveling, he receives a few hundred people in the courtyard of his residence in Dharamsala. On one such morning, the Dalai Lama spotted me, camera in hand, standing next to his official photographer. "Who are you?" he asked. I explained I was born in China, escaped after the Communist takeover, and grew up in Japan. I told him I had been photographing the Tibetan diaspora for a decade. He gave me a heartwarming smile and said, "I want to meet you privately," and asked one of his secretaries to organize this meeting. Then he continued to greet the long line of people. There were Bhutanese students, Mongolian nuns, Westerners, and Indians, and as my trip coincided with the Tibetan New Year, there were also numerous Tibetans who had come from all over the world to visit their families in the settlements and to attend the Dalai Lama's teaching. Some cried, some glowed as if touched by light, and some had stories to tell. Even when visibly tired after meeting 500 people, the Dalai Lama listened intently and spoke with kindness. He often took people's hands or put his arm around their shoulder. He smiled and laughed throughout this public session. There were some groups I couldn't photograph for political reasons.

Over the course of the few weeks I spent in Dharamsala, during the Tibetan New Year, I had the privilege of being in close proximity to the Dalai Lama as he went about his business—ordaining monks and nuns, giving teachings, meeting Tibetans and non-Tibetans, being interviewed by the Indian press, and attending the Mind and Life Dialogue. The Dalai Lama generously invited me to observe centuries-old traditions, then granted me the rare opportunity to interview him one on one, and an even rarer privilege to photograph him in his private residence while he meditated. During this time, the Dalai Lama never changed. He is who he is—authentic, transparent, sincere, kind, and compassionate.

Few leaders move from good to great. Some leaders become great in crisis, but once the crisis is over, they fail as leaders. The Dalai Lama didn't prepare for leadership; he was simply born into the role. His leadership is by birthright. He was recognized and identified as the reincarnate 14th Dalai Lama. Having birthright credibility does not make a good leader. When at the age of twenty-four, he fled Lhasa and began his journey to freedom, he didn't envision that 85,000 Tibetans would follow him into exile. What he made from this tragic experience—resettling his people in settlements where they can have a livelihood, establishing separate Tibetan schools for the children to safeguard their culture, reestablishing cultural and religious institutions such as the Tibetan Library and the monasteries—makes him an incredible leader. He gained the trust, respect, and love of his people by sharing the same tragic experiences as them. He was given power, but he does not lead from power.

The Dalai Lama is one of the greatest Buddhist scholars, practitioners, teachers, and spiritual leaders of our times. He leads from inner truth, motivation, and sincerity. He promotes universal human values and integrity. What makes him great is his readiness to respond when a situation arises that demands the best of him. The Dalai Lama found his footing in Tibet's crisis, and when the crisis stabilized, he traveled the world to learn from it. When he saw that material comfort did not bring happiness, he felt the Tibetan culture of compassion, non-violence, and peace would be beneficial to the world. This led him to develop his vision for a universal ethics grounded in kindness and compassion, both insights from Buddhist teachings, and he has been sharing this with the world through his writings and teachings.

The Dalai Lama's towering intellect enables him to see from a broad, holistic, and strategic perspective, and his deep spirituality has given him a moral stature that few world leaders have earned. His openness, love of people, and charisma have propelled him onto a global leadership platform. He has no formal position or power, yet when he addresses the issues and challenges we face today—human rights, civil rights, poverty, and environmental crisis—he helps us to look beyond our small world and inspires us to action. And when the whole world is in chaos and turmoil, his message to us is not only caring, calming, and appreciative, but he tells us we can each make a difference by reaching out to one another with compassion and wisdom. And, by working together, we can create a peaceful and more egalitarian world. His greatness is his sincerity, motivation, and generosity, which contribute to bringing inner peace of mind and true happiness to humanity. As a global citizen and leader, he is a beacon of light—shining a vision of what we can be as people and as communities.

Photo by Bonnie Brooks

THE AUTHOR'S STORY

Sitting in a darkened theater watching a scene from the movie *Julia*, where Lillian Hellman, played by Jane Fonda, is smuggling large sums of money into pre-war Germany, the tension I felt during Lillian's long train ride was so unbearable that I ran out of the cinema for fresh air. I was so shaken; I informed the ticket seller there should have been a warning about how frightening this movie is. She assured me no one else had ever complained, but, nonetheless, gave me a refund. Years later, when I told my mother about the scene in the movie, she said, "How do you remember the train ride? You were only three years old." I realized then that the movie was depicting our own refugee experience. I am fortunate—my father wrote his biography before he died, and my mother has since written hers. Many refugees are reluctant to tell their children about their experiences, perhaps it is too painful to relive them by telling their stories.

In November 1951, two years after the Communist Party's takeover of China, my twenty-three-year-old mother, who is half Japanese and half indigenous Chinese, boarded a train from Beijing with three small children ranging in age from four months to three and a half years. I was the three-and-a-half-year-old. To this day, I remember the terror and anxiety as the People's Liberation Army (PLA) soldiers came hourly to interrogate my mother during the long train journey from Beijing in north China to Guangdong in southern China. "Where are you going with your children? Where is your husband?" She would reply, "I don't know where my husband is. I am going to Guangdong to find him."

My father, who was already in Hong Kong, had learned that formal channels to obtain a visa weren't working, and so he went to Macau, a Portuguese territory until 1999, where the borders were never closed, to meet us. This would be the first time he would see his newborn son. From Macau, we climbed into the cargo hold of a small fishing boat along with other refugees. In the chaos and confusion, I was separated from my parents and thrown onto another boat, which, of course, terrified me into a panic and a crying fit. Fearing for the others, one of the adults gagged me with a dirty rag and tried to push me into the river. My father was able to grab me from the adjacent boat and sit me between himself and my mother so that I quieted down. I don't remember crying after that. We safely arrived in New Territories, where we hitchhiked to Hong Kong. We settled in Hong Kong, where I attended a Cantonese nursery school. Two years later, in 1953, my family made another journey, this time legally, by cargo ship to Japan where I grew up. In Tokyo, I was enrolled in a Japanese kindergarten. I remember feeling frustrated at trying to communicate without success and Japanese boys throwing pebbles at me. After one unhappy year, my parents decided to send all three of us to an International elementary school; by the time I was six years old, I was learning my fourth language.

In 1971, the United Nations General Assembly admitted the People's Republic of China (PRC) and expelled the Republic of China (Taiwan); Communist China assumed Taiwan's place in the General Assembly as well as its place as one of the five permanent members of the United Nations. Eight years later, President Nixon visited China and normalized relations between the USA and China. Chinese refugees were living perilously in Japan because they were only given short term visas lasting anywhere from three months to three years. During this time, my family emigrated to the United States, as did many other Chinese refugees. My mother has expressed her tremendous gratitude that we could call the United States our home. Years later, when interviewing the Tibetan refugees who fled from Tibet to Nepal, then to India and to North America, I heard them echo the same sentiment.

Sacred mantra carved in stone.

THE DALAI LAMA'S STORY: ESCAPE

Tibet stands in the heart of Central Eurasia with the Himalaya Mountains to the south, the Kunlun Mountains to the north, the Hindu Kush range to the west, and the Great Wall of China to the east. Since the seventeenth century, Tibetans have lived in relative peace as they pursued the spiritual path of their adopted Buddhist religion. Living at an average elevation of 3 miles (5,000 meters) above sea level, they have been able to maintain their ancient culture, protected by their geographic isolation.

The world is so familiar with the charismatic Dalai Lama and his contagious laughter, we take who he is for granted. The 14th Dalai Lama is the only Dalai Lama who has become a leader of global importance. In today's world, there are few hereditary leaders, leaders by birthright. Uniquely, the Dalai Lama is the only reincarnate world leader, a leader whose role was discovered when he was a child. In a Buddhist monastic society, where celibacy is the rule, reincarnation ensured the continuity of political and spiritual hierarchy. The title, Dalai Lama, is unique to Tibetan Buddhism. The first living bearer of the title was the Third Dalai Lama Sonam Gyatso (1543–1588), the spiritual advisor to Altan Khan, the Mongolian King. The First and Second Dalai Lamas were named posthumously. The first four Dalai Lamas had no political authority. The Fifth Dalai Lama (1617–1682) was the first Dalai Lama to have simultaneously both political and spiritual authority in Tibet. Subsequent Dalai Lamas either did not live to adulthood or had very little power. The thirteenth Dalai Lama (1876–1933), however, was a visionary and saw the need for progress. He lived at a time of global upheaval surrounding Tibet and wanted to build a military, but his calls for arms were to no avail. Tibet had been disarmed for over 300 years, and the people refused to change. Although it was predicted that the 13th Dalai Lama would live to an old age, he chose to die earlier at middle age for his reincarnation to reach adulthood in time to cope with the tragedy that he had foreseen.

The 14th Dalai Lama was born into a family of farmers on July 6, 1935, in Amdo, East Tibet. How this child, named Lhamo Thondup, was identified as the reincarnate of the 13th Dalai Lama may be a familiar story. Briefly, when he was not quite three years old, a search party that had followed several signs and visions seen by the Regent arrived at his family's house. The leader of the party pretended to be a servant only to be uncovered by the little boy who identified who he really was. He also recognized all the belongings of the 13th Dalai Lama and insisted they were his. Before the young child could go to Lhasa, the capital of Tibet, the governor who had control of that region, a non-Tibetan, demanded an exorbitant amount of money. The young child was moved to Kumbum Monastery until funds could be raised. Separated from his parents and his siblings, the Dalai Lama refers to those months in his autobiography[1] as being very lonely. Freed only after the ransom was paid, he and his family made the long three-month journey to Lhasa. When he arrived, they took him and his older brother to Norbulingka, the summer Palace, instead of the austere Potala Palace. His carefree life at Norbulingka, however, quickly ended when he was moved, alone, to the austere Potala Palace, the seat of spiritual and political authority in Tibet. There he was enthroned as spiritual leader of Tibet and was ordained as a novice monk and given a new name—Jetsun Jamphel Ngawang Lobsang Yeshe Tenzin Gyatso. His education focused exclusively on Buddhist studies: he meditated, studied writings, and memorized Buddhist scripture, very much like any other monk.

The Dalai Lama was kept in the dark about almost everything, including news about the Chinese from the Regent placed in charge until he became of age. His childhood would have been unbearably isolating if it were not for the sweepers who cleaned the Palace. They told the Dalai Lama everything he wanted to know. Standing on a chest, he would peek through a glass partition, which separated his room from the Regent's room. One day, he saw a messenger running to the Palace. He knew something was wrong because news was brought to the Regent once weekly, and he had already received that week's news. The Dalai Lama's suspicion was confirmed when he saw the Regent's disturbed face as he read that urgent message. Days later, he was told that Chinese soldiers had invaded Eastern Tibet.

In 1949, when the Dalai Lama was fourteen years old, Mao Zedong swept to power and established the People's Republic of China. He announced the liberation of Tibet was one of his priorities. Within a year, 80,000 PLA soldiers crossed the Drichu (Yangtze) River and invaded Eastern Tibet. When the political situation worsened, the Tibetan people demanded that the Dalai Lama be given full temporal power. One of the overriding weaknesses of reincarnation is that regents are in charge until the reincarnate reaches maturity. This situation often results in political conflict between factions wanting control, as it happened in this case. The Dalai Lama wrote in his autobiography that he hadn't yet completed his Buddhist studies, wasn't educated in leadership, and didn't have knowledge about the wider world. Kept in the dark about state affairs, he felt ill prepared, but he knew the Tibetan people trusted only him. Out of a sense of duty and service to his country, at the age of fifteen, three years earlier than the designated time, the Dalai Lama was ordained the supreme spiritual and temporal ruler of Tibet. The situation in Tibet was so dire that soon after his investiture, the Dalai Lama was taken incognito to Dromo, a small Tibetan village in Yatung, close to the Sikkim border. From there he could flee to India should it become necessary. A Chinese General assigned to Lhasa nonetheless tracked him down and insisted on paying a visit. The Dalai Lama told me about the General's visit.

> *This is a strange story. On July 16, 1951, General Zhang Jinwu, the Chinese representative in Lhasa, came to my place. Before entering my room in the monastery, my older brother Lobsang Samten peeked and exclaimed, "The Chinese communist is also a human being!" We had the impression the communists were demons.*

The Dalai Lama laughed, then told me that after he realized that the Chinese General was a human being like himself, and not a devil, it had a lasting impact on him. He vowed that from then on, he would investigate through personal observation rather than coming to uninformed conclusions.

Before he left Lhasa, the Dalai Lama had sent a delegation to negotiate with the Chinese. Under duress and without authorization they agreed to sign the Seventeen-Point Agreement, affirming China's sovereignty over Tibet. The Chinese falsified this agreement with a forged state seal. When the General arrived, he gave a copy of the Agreement to the Dalai Lama. The Dalai Lama continued with his story in a very serious tone:

> *General Zhang gave me a copy of the Seventeen-Point Agreement and two supplementary documents. One of the documents indicated: in the case of the Dalai Lama escaping to India, the door would be open for him to come back to Tibet. What this meant was, whenever I return, I am welcome, so don't bother to leave. The second document indicated that the Tibetan army eventually should become part of the Liberation army.*

After a nine-month stay in Dromo, the Dalai Lama traveled back to Lhasa in an elaborate style, stopping at villages along the way to meet the local people and to give Buddhist teachings. He wanted to demonstrate to his people, most likely in anticipation of future hardship, that the practice of Buddhism is relevant no matter what the circumstance. By the time the Dalai Lama returned to Lhasa, in 1951, the Chinese officials and troops were already stationed there. Tibet was in crisis—disputes, food shortages, rebellion—all of which created massive chaos. (It was around this time my family was escaping from Beijing to Hong Kong.)

While trying to calm the situation, the Dalai Lama set up a reform committee to make changes. He wanted to establish an independent judiciary, develop a system of universal education, and build roads—all of which required long-term planning. The Dalai Lama explained why he wanted to reform the Tibetan government.

> *The Tibet government had drawbacks—mainly power in a few people's hands. In 1952, I set up a reform committee to carry out some change. Since my childhood I had some aspirations about democracy. Then, I was totally against the feudal system and was fed up with it. I had inspirations for democracy, liberty, socialism.*

Contrary to the terms of the Seventeen-Point Agreement, which made it clear that Tibet could carry out its own reforms, the Chinese Government started to introduce collective farming, starting in Amdo. The Dalai Lama was powerless and could only implement a partial land reform. He abolished the system of inheritable debt and wrote off all government loans that could not be repaid. The Dalai Lama tried to find a workable solution, and at the invitation of Chairman Mao, he went to Beijing in 1954 to work things out.

At first, the Dalai Lama was impressed with the progress the Chinese government had made. Mao, who was sixty-one years old and fully in power, treated the nineteen-year-old Dalai Lama as an honored guest, although that special treatment had its drawbacks, as the Dalai Lama explained:

> *Mao Zedong and I became very close friends. One funny thing— whenever there was some banquet, Mao always called me to sit by him. In Chinese tradition, the host picks up food with his chopsticks and places it on the plate of the honored guest. In one way I felt honored, but in another not. Chairman Mao was always coughing. Oh, those germs in my stomach!*

Mao seemed to have taken to the young Dalai Lama, and, in turn, the Dalai Lama said he felt they had mutual trust. They met privately several times with just their respective interpreters.

> There were several private meetings with Mao where only our translators, one Tibetan and one Liberation Army representative, were present. We trusted each other. We firmly believed that under Communist China leadership, Tibet could be developed. I received this as wonderful advice. He really treated me as his own son, and I considered him my father.

The Dalai Lama was, obviously, searching for alternative models of government to replace the Tibetan model. He continued:

> With my discussion with Chairman Mao, I told him I totally really admired Marxism. Even today, as far as social economic theory is concerned, I am Marxist. That wonderful ideology, I think, was spoiled by Lenin. That also is understandable. When the 1917 Bolshevik Revolution took place, besides the civil war, the Western attitude was also more negative. As a result, Lenin's mind became more militant—during war tight control, ruthless control, and secrecy—these practices in war time could be relevant [to those who wanted to uphold the status quo]. So, this wonderful theory was mainly meant for working class people with its principles of democracy and not for a few royals trying to lead an entire nation. Then eventually, because of circumstances, Lenin created some kind of totalitarian system. Then Stalin came and further tightened control.

One day, while attending the Steering Committee of the People's National Congress of PRC, of which he served as a Vice President, Mao unexpectedly sent for him. Unable to find his interpreter, the Dalai Lama went with his bodyguard instead. First, Mao advised him on leadership skills—how to organize and listen to different people's ideas. As a keen learner, the Dalai Lama thought the advice was "wonderful." Then, Mao said something that exposed his true feelings towards religion. The Dalai Lama recalled the shocking incident and said he listened with disbelief:

Mao then came closer to me and said, "Your mind is very scientific, so religion is opium." I was more than a little bit shocked and tried to avoid showing my face to Mao by focusing on taking notes.

It showed he trusted me. But, where religion is concerned, that was difficult to accept. I am Dalai Lama, a Buddhist monk. To a Buddhist monk is religion poison?

He accompanied me to the car, opened the door and I got in. He closed the door and waved as we drove away. He was very friendly.

The Dalai Lama continued with a mischievous smile:

If Mao were still alive, I am quite sure he would say Buddhism is an exception. Buddhism is not faith but the training of mind through reasoning!

It was the last time the two met. By the time the Dalai Lama returned to Lhasa, the situation had deteriorated; fighting had started in East Tibet and thousands of refugees were camped in Lhasa. The Chinese propaganda directed at him didn't last long. The Dalai Lama concluded the Chinese had also become corrupt; they weren't helping to modernize Tibet at all. Despite his lack of leadership education, the Dalai Lama showed a natural capacity for leadership. His heightened observational skills honed from years of looking through the divide in the room to see what the Regent was doing, his curiosity to learn new things, his analytical skills, and his ability to adapt to new data came naturally to him and became essential to his leadership role. The Dalai Lama reflected:

I think the Chinese communist in the early period in Yunang followed democratic principles. In 1954, when I visited different places, I was meeting with party members as well as nonparty members. When I met with people, we discussed real problems. I was very impressed with party members as they were really dedicated. So, while I was in Beijing, I suggested to some officials that I wanted to join the Chinese Community Party. They said, no hurry. Eventually the Chinese communist party became rotten. That was in 1954–55.

In 1956, the Dalai Lama visited India and met with Pandit Nehru, who invited him to attend a session of the Indian Parliament. The Dalai Lama was impressed with the freedom of the Indian officials to criticize the Prime Minister. He saw democracy at work and was impressed by it.

Despite the threatening and desperate situation in Tibet, the Dalai Lama was able to concentrate on his Buddhist studies for the next two years. The major subjects included logic, fine arts, Sanskrit, and medicine, with the greatest emphasis on Buddhist philosophy.

In 1957, I was busy studying. We set the year of my final exam for 1959. For two years I studied quite seriously—one way study.

His final examination consisted of delivering a series of dialectical debates before an audience of 10,000 monks. Upon achieving the Geshe Lharampa degree (Doctor of Buddhist Philosophy), Dalai Lama left Jokhang Temple in grandeur. Thousands of Tibetans lined the four-mile-long route between the temple and Potala. Unbeknown to them, it was the last time such a full pageantry would be on display and was, for most of them, the last time they would see the Dalai Lama.

A few days later, at the pretext of celebrating his graduation, General Tan invited the Dalai Lama to see a play, but strangely, asked him not to bring his bodyguards with him. Word of this leaked out. The Tibetans were convinced the Chinese were going to kidnap their beloved leader. All the Tibetan women in Lhasa got together to protest by blocking the gates.

The Dalai Lama tells the story leading up to his escape from Lhasa and him ultimately seeking asylum in India:

On March 10, 1959, things became really explosive. I had been invited to see a play that day. On that very day, I think almost 10,000 Tibetans from Lhasa came to Norbulingka and blocked all the gates. They wouldn't allow me out to see the play. I sent some senior officials to meet General Tan Guansan to say I was unable to attend. Over the course of a week, I tried my best to cool down the situation. I met some representatives and told them a few could stay but others should leave. They didn't listen to me!

The Chinese General must not have believed the Dalai Lama when he said he could not control the crowd. This would never have happened in China. The General plainly did not understand that the Dalai Lama belonged to the people!

The Tibetans were justified in their suspicion. The Dalai Lama continued with his story:

> In the meantime, each night, the Chinese troops moved in with big guns. One day we noticed that the sixteen or so artillery emplacements which were set up opposite the Potala were uncovered. I heard the explosion of two artillery rounds. Finally, the Oracle, who had originally said, "the Dalai Lama should remain," said, "Now the time has come. Go!" I think he left it to the last moment so the secret of my departure wouldn't get out.

The Dalai Lama's mother, older sister, and younger brother left in the first group disguised as soldiers. The Dalai Lama followed with his two tutors and several Cabinet members in the second group. After crossing the Tsangpo River in boats made from animal skins, horses awaited them. The Dalai Lama recollected that fearful night so vividly, I found myself sitting on the edge of the sofa.

> On March 17, at 10 pm Lhasa time, we left Norbulingka, my palace. I was dressed as an ordinary Tibetan soldier and carried a rifle. The officials were also dressed as soldiers. Phala, the Lord Chamberlain, and Gadrang Lobsang Tenzin went ahead to check the guard gate. After the two officials had safely passed the gate, I followed. I had worn glasses since 1954, but I could not wear glasses as an ordinary soldier. I found it a little difficult to walk at night. For a few moments I was their assistant. After crossing the gate and the river, I then became the boss, and they became my assistants.

> They had already arranged some horses. The river was towards the west and the Chinese military camp was in the north. There were some people on the other side of the river. We could see they were Chinese soldiers with guns. None of us used flashlights, but we could not stop the sound of horses' hoofs. At that moment there was real danger. I became quite fearful.

Around 1 am we reached a place where we had a short rest. Then we continued on horseback. The next morning, we came close to Che-La pass. There, my horse and I turned north towards the Lhasa Valley and Potala Palace for one last look.

I felt saddened when he said he took one last look at Lhasa Valley. I glanced at the Dalai Lama but couldn't tell what he was feeling.

The Dalai Lama had planned to repudiate the Seventeen-Point Agreement, reestablish the Tibetan government, and open negotiations with the Chinese when he arrived in Lhuntse Dzong, close to the Indian border. However, forty-eight hours after his escape, the PLA shelled the Norbulingka and Potala Palaces and unleashed a military crackdown in Lhasa. On March 28, 1959, Zhou Enlai, head of Communist China, announced China's annexation of Tibet and the dissolution of the Tibetan government. The Dalai Lama's hope for coexistence completely shattered; he formally repudiated the Seventeen-Point Agreement and announced the formation of his own government. He had no option but to seek asylum in India. He sent a small party of the fittest men to cross into India to warn the Indian officials that he was planning to seek asylum. The men returned shortly afterwards with the news that the Indian government had given permission for asylum. Exhausted and ill, the Dalai Lama reached the Indian border on March 31, 1959. The Dalai Lama was just twenty-four years old.

Photo courtesy of the Office of the Dalai Lama

THE DALAI LAMA'S STORY: LEADER OF THE TIBETANS

I listened, absorbed, as the Dalai Lama told me his story of escape. He has retold this story many times, but it still sounded fresh. His sharp and retentive mind recollects dates, names, and places. Just before he got to the part where he was requesting asylum in India he paused, noticed I had not touched my tea, and said, "Drink, drink your tea." Then continued with his narrative. That gesture of a good host jolted me back to the twenty-first century. I was surprised how fluid and attentive the Dalai Lama was—easily moving from being a gracious host to telling his gripping narrative.

> *End of part one, my escape and beginning of part two, our survival. After reaching India, a large number of refugees followed me. My immediate task was to look after them.*

When the Dalai Lama reached India, he was first given temporary housing in Mussoorie, a hill station near Delhi. Prime Minister Pandit Jawaharlal Nehru soon visited and gave him invaluable advice. The following day, the Dalai Lama met with the senior Tibetan officials who had either escaped with him or had arrived earlier, reestablished the Tibetan Government-in-exile, and started to plan for the immediate as well the long-term requirements for the refugees. Organization came about because the Dalai Lama saw its importance. It wasn't by chance that he escaped with his key government officials and advisors. He quickly formed an organization to manage the basic human needs for the constant flow of refugees. The Dalai Lama and his government met in Bodh Gaya, a holy place where Buddha was enlightened over 2,500 years ago. There, they laid the foundation for a democracy which incorporated values from Tibetan culture. The Dalai Lama explained:

> *We started to work on reforming our departments and officials. Then, in 1960, we started working for democratization in Bodh Gaya, at a meeting of representatives. We decided to draft a constitution, with the help of the people's representatives.*

The Dalai Lama did not expect 85,000 Tibetans to follow him to India. He put aside his initial plan to win independence for Tibet to solve the enormous challenge of taking care of the health and safety of the refugees. The refugees were initially sent to one of two transit camps in lower elevations. The climate was hot and humid, conditions to which the high-plateau Tibetans were unaccustomed. Many were overcome by tuberculosis and heat stroke. Fearful that many more would die if they were left there, the Dalai Lama appealed to Prime Minister Nehru to move the Tibetans to cooler elevations. Those who survived were assigned to build road in the high Himalayan foothills in Sikkim, Kalimpong, Darjeeling, and Shillong. Men, women, and children worked alongside each other, carrying rocks, breaking them into smaller pieces, and then placing them to build roads. They lived in makeshift tents, moving from place to place as the roads were built. A Tibetan woman I interviewed recalled how her mother sang to help her through the day doing work that Tibetans, mostly nomads and farmers, were unsuited to do. "My mother and the women sang continuously—when they left the house early in the morning, during the grueling work, and when they walked home. Singing kept them alive," she said.

Tibetans attending the Dalai Lama's teaching, Tsuglagkhang Courtyard.

First Tibetan school, Mussoorie

EDUCATING THE FUTURE

A month after exile, the Indian Government assigned the Dalai Lama a "permanent home" in McLeod Ganj, a suburb of Dharamsala, a deserted British hill station 292 miles from Delhi. It is situated in the Dhauladhar range, part of the Himalayan chain of mountains. He first shared a bungalow with his mother and later, his sister and her two young children moved in as well. Jetsun Pema recalls her brother constantly studying, even during meals. In Tibet, protocol prevented the Dalai Lama from interacting with ordinary Tibetans. In exile he liked to walk freely among his people. He found that children suffered the most—many had arrived sick from their hazardous escape while others were injured by falling rocks on the road building sites. When he moved to Dharamsala, he immediately entrusted his elder sister, Tsering Dolma, to start a nursery for both orphans and children who were separated from their families during their escape. Initially, fifty-one children arrived from the road construction camps. Dozens more arrived daily until, at one point, 120 children shared a single room. Within a short time, thousands of children were smuggled out of Tibet and placed in the Dalai Lama's care. Tibetans continued to risk their lives to bring some of their children to India, only to go back to Tibet to care for other members of the family. Tsering told me her father escaped with her and her brother, then went back to Tibet to care for the ten children left behind. This practice only stopped when Nepal closed its borders to Tibet.

Jetsun Pema, the Dalai Lama's younger sister, took over the school upon her sister's untimely death. The Tibetan Children's Village (TCV) grew into full-fledged schools under her forty-two-year directorship. Jetsun Pema, whom I met in Dharamsala, explained the beginnings of the TCV and its organic growth. In the early days of exile, it provided a home for orphans and children from destitute families. Initially, the main intent was simply to feed the undernourished children and protect them from harm's way. Over time, the TCV grew into a school. Jetsun Pema explained the vulnerable situation of the children.

> *When I came to Dharamsala my sister was involved with the children. Those children were the ones who escaped with their parents from Tibet. The only kind of work the Government of India could give them was road construction in the mountain regions.*

*The Tibetans who escaped were mostly farmers and nomads. So
when they came to India, there was no work for them: there was
no land for them to farm and there were no animals to look after.
The Indian Government sent them in batches to regions in Ladakh,
Manali, and Himachal Pradesh to construct roads.*

*His Holiness heard of the plight of children along the construction
sites, and he said to collect these children and bring them to
Dharamsala. From Jammu there were fifty-one children. He
entrusted the children to my sister. That is how TCV initially started.*

*When the parents had nothing, I suppose it was a very difficult
task for the parents to take care of their children and feed them
properly. So, when the children were taken away, it was a great
relief for the parents. At the construction sites they were always
dynamiting the rocks causing them to roll down hillside which was
dangerous for the children. Sending the children to Dharamsala was
a great help to the children.*

Jetsun Pema felt the children had suffered so much during their flight from
Tibet that they required special attention and care. Some of the children had
seen their parents die or taken away by Chinese soldiers. Others had an arm or
leg amputated due to frostbite during their escape. To safeguard the mental and
emotional well-being of the children who had suffered unimaginable trauma, a
group of family homes, each with a house "mother" to look after the children,
were set up. The first house was built in 1967 and twenty-five children moved in.

*The main purpose of the house was to provide a loving home
in which to bring up Tibetan children; to give them parents who
would take care of them. These children grew up in a real family
atmosphere. First, we took care of their needs—food, shelter, and
clothing—then their education.*

Mothers hold an important and valued position in Tibetan culture. In his
teachings, the Dalai Lama tells us to treat everyone with compassion and
kindness, adding that that person could have been our mother in our past lives!

Buddhists believe in the continuity of life and rebirth, called reincarnation, based on the continuity of the mind. The Dalai Lama has said many times how kind and compassionate his mother was, not only to her family, but to everyone. He credits her for planting the seed of compassion in him. It is therefore predictable to discover that, along with the teachers, the women who manage the TCV's houses called "mothers" play a prominent role in the education and welfare of the students. The mothers are professionally trained to manage the homes and to provide the children with emotional and social care. Their training includes Buddhism, psychology, health, nutrition, hygiene, management of the homes, and environmental awareness. These mothers could be married and have their own children; however, their own families do not live with them at the TCV.

I have met many TCV alumni in India, Nepal, and in the USA. One of the TCV alumni cooks meals for visitors who stay at the settlement guest house in Bylakuppe. One evening, when she brought over a delicious Tibetan meal, she told me how the TCV saved her life. She said her parents had escaped with her older brother. Both she and her younger brother were born in India at a road construction site. Her parents were one of the first to work on the road, and there

TCV "mother" in front of a home that houses about thirty students.

was a lot of dynamiting. When her father was killed by falling rocks, her mother lost her mind and was unable to care for her children. She and her brothers were sent to the TCV with a small stipend from His Holiness' sister.

Pandit Nehru anticipated the Tibetan refugees would be guests of India for the foreseeable future and agreed with the Dalai Lama that educating the children in their own schools was crucial to the survival of Tibetan culture. Soon after the refugees arrived in India, the Central Tibetan Schools Administration (CTSA) was created within the Indian Ministry of Education specifically for the purpose of educating the Tibetan children. The first Tibetan school was established by the Indian government in Mussoorie, less than a year after exile, with four teachers and fifty eager students.

As more children fled Tibet and arrived in India, additional schools were built to accommodate them. And then, as the children grew older, higher grades were added. In this way, TCV grew organically to accommodate the needs of the situation. Jetsun Pema continued with her story:

> *Fortunately, the Government of India by then had opened four*
> *residential schools where the older children were sent. The younger*

ones were raised in the TCV in Dharamsala. Each year more children came. Soon the Indian government schools were full, and they couldn't take any more children. The older children remained in TCV and that's when we started schooling from grades one and two and so on. And, over the years, it went all the way up through high school.

I asked Jetsun Pema how the two school systems differed. She said:

CTS follows rules set by the Indian Government and we are very grateful. At TCV we always felt teaching the Tibetan children was a service to the nation. And as the years went by, the children who had graduated from the school came back as teachers, nurses, or staff. Their feeling towards the children and their work there makes a lot of difference.

Jetsun Pema said that whenever the Dalai Lama visits the TCV, he reaffirms some aspects of Tibetan cultural values. He wants to ensure the children develop Tibetan values of peace and nonviolence. On one occasion, he wanted the

children to understand the values of gratitude and kindness and spoke to that effect. "Others before self" became the motto for the TCV. She elaborated on this when she said:

> His Holiness came to TCV in 1972 and gave a talk. He said, "Remember, you are being educated, fed, and living through the kindness of other people. You have received benefits. When you leave this place, you have to think about how you can benefit others." As a result, "others before self" is our motto. Teachers explain what this means to all new children who come here.

Jetsun Pema described how the Dalai Lama has inspired and motivated the teachers to keep creating an educationally stimulating environment for the children.

> In our case, I must say, mostly we are grateful to His Holiness' vision. Whenever His Holiness came and talked with the children, we always reflected on what he said and discussed how we could carry out his wishes. We have the liberty to bring about changes. I think in the field of education there are basics—love, compassion, tender care—those are things that will always remain.

Under the Dalai Lama's encouragement, Jetsun Pema and the teachers experimented with many modern educational models; however, the Tibetan culture, with its foundation of compassion, non-violence, and peace always remains at the core. Language is one of the most important aspects of a culture. In the 1980s it was decided that TCV would replace English with Tibetan as the primary language. The syllabus for the primary school was translated from English to Tibetan and new Tibetan subjects were added. Many of the teachers feared the students would be left behind when they transferred to a middle school that followed the Indian curriculum, and the subjects are taught in English. Jetsun Pema said, fortunately, their fears were unfounded. The teachers discovered that when the children were taught in their mother tongue, their understanding increased, and they asked more questions.

> By asking more questions they came to build self-confidence. With more self-confidence they are more at peace with themselves. There was more discipline. The learning was more enthusiastic from

the children. After four to five years, the teachers realized this was a good thing. In middle school, English was taught as a second language. Since children's understanding was good, there was no problem in switching over.

I think that was the biggest contribution to Tibetan education. The children have a good foundation in the Tibetan language. Written and spoken language is the foundation for any culture. Even if we are refugees and we don't have our own country, we have our identity. And wherever you are, you have a bit of Tibetan in you.

The Tibetan schools in India and Nepal continue to serve the original two purposes—to provide a modern education alongside studies in Tibetan language, culture, history, and religion. Education in the Tibetan schools acknowledges the need to care for each student's mental, physical, and emotional well-being as well

Classes are taught in Tibetan.

as providing students with the knowledge and skills required to function and live responsibly. In short, the objectives of the Tibetan education system are to ensure every child can stand on his or her own feet and contribute to the community, and to develop a sense of national pride and identity. It is a holistic approach to educating children. According to Jetsun Pema:

> His Holiness always insisted that while we are in exile, the best thing we can do is to educate the children. We felt that implementing His Holiness' vision was our big responsibility. We tried to give the children the best modern education we could by learning from others and taking the best from all over the world.
>
> But in the back of our minds, we never forget that these are Tibetan children growing up in a foreign land. Whatever we do with modern education, we believe that we must keep them rooted in their Tibetan culture and make them aware that they are Buddhists. We must give them the best modern education but also never forget our ancient culture and history. So, for Tibetan children growing up in exile, we try to give them both so that in the end they are proud to be Tibetans.

Tibetan children in the TCV develop as Tibetans. At the beginning and end of the school day, the entire school gathers for the recitation of prayers, often led by a monk. In the classrooms, the walls are filled with student artwork depicting Tibet culture, a map of Tibet, paintings of the Potala Palace and photographs of the Dalai Lama. Students participate in school-sponsored special cultural exhibitions, dancing, drama, singing, and sports competitions. I observed a debate between a group of monks and students which was intense and fun and almost as vivid as the often-theatrical debate among monks. Students actively participate in important celebrations such as the Losar (New Year), Tibetan Uprising Day, and the Dalai Lama's birthday.

The Tibetan educational principle of awakening and developing the qualities of wisdom, loving kindness, and compassion is visible. In many of the younger classes, the children sang Chinese songs when they were told I was born in China and English songs when they were told I was visiting from London. I was repeatedly struck by their happy faces and enthusiasm. When it was time to go outdoors, classmates who were more able helped the younger ones to tie their shoes before putting on their own shoes. Back in the classrooms, children helped each other with reading and tracing the Tibetan alphabet. These spontaneous acts of kindness were heartwarming to see. The school's motto, "others before self," is consistently demonstrated.

The TCV homes are not dormitories, but family homes. These homes are self-contained—each has their own kitchen, laundry, and other facilities. There is a prayer room and a bedroom for girls and one for boys. The day that I visited it was washing and cleaning day, and some of the children did the laundry while others polished shoes. One little girl stood in a large tin bucket so as not to get her shoes wet while she hosed her "sister's" soapy hair. The older children were chopping vegetables. Dolker Dorje said when she first entered the TCV as a toddler, she was taught to count the number of spoons. As she grew older, she was given more responsibility from an older student who showed her the new task. In this way, she learned to wash, peel, cut, and cook vegetables! Even after graduating from TCV, the children who grew up in the same homes continue to stay in touch with each other regardless of where they live in the world.

In addition to academic education, Tibetan children attending TCV are taught tools for creating a peaceful society. In one of the TCVs, I noticed a clearly marked area planted with flowers. When children argue with each other, they go to this special area fittingly named, the "Zone of Peace." There they stay awhile, reflect about what they are fighting about, discuss the situation with each other and then make peace and shake hands. A zone of peace is found in each of the homes and on TCV campuses. Although retired for over a decade, Jetsun Pema spoke passionately about the TCV as if she was sitting in her office with the teachers and students. "*The children don't play with guns or swords or war games. Peace has left an imprint on the TCV educated children,*" Jetsun Pema happily concluded. No doubt the Zone of Peace is motivated by the Dalai Lama's unwavering commitment to non-violence.

The TCV is such a compelling educational model, even Tibetans who live in the West still seek to enroll their children there. Kalsang and Dolker Dorje are two such Tibetans. They visited Dharamsala during the Losar celebration and had come to visit their parents and to enroll their two sons, ages nine and eleven, in the TCV for two years. They said their American friends could not understand why they would take their sons out of one of the top schools in California to send them to the TCV. Husband and wife reminisced about their happy memories of growing up in the TCV. Dolker said they had no toys— for fun, they would race up the water tower. They said that while the boys' school in the USA has a strong curriculum for intellectual development, it is missing spiritual values. Through the Dalai Lama's influence, the TCV focuses on educating the heart as well as the mind. Children are educated to become responsible human beings. Their sons were placed in a special language class along with other Tibetans who live in the west. Once they strengthen their language skills, they will be assigned to the proper grade for their age. When the parents visited their sons the next day, the two boys had already made friends with a Tibetan boy from New York who was showing them the ropes. Their preschool three-year-old daughter wanted to stay with her brothers. Her parents promised to bring her back when she got older.

When I was sequencing the story of the Tibetan diaspora, Rinchen Dharlo, President Emeritus of the Tibet Fund, who generated my itinerary and guided me throughout this project, told me that the Dalai Lama built schools before he built the settlements—that's how important education is to him. The Dalai Lama was aware that without establishing their own schools to preserve Tibetan culture and

language, the children would be absorbed into Indian culture. He responded right away to the suffering of the children and took care of them first. In his conviction that the survival of Tibetan culture and way of life depends on the children, he placed their care first with his elder sister, and at her untimely death, with his younger sister. He explained what he wanted, delegated responsibilities, and then provided resources and support. He made sure everybody was doing what was required of them. This delegation of authority of such an important project attests to the Dalai Lama's high regard for women.

Before the Chinese incursion, schools for the general population were scarce in Tibet. In exile, the first Tibetan School in India was established just a few months into exile, and by 1964, there were residential schools in Dharamsala, schools in the settlements, and transit schools even at road construction sites. Later, when many young adults escaped to India, vocational schools were added. The Dalai Lama's vision to provide secular modern education for the Tibetan children resulted in nearly 100% literacy rate within a generation.

Tibetans carry their traditions with them and project them far beyond any geographic boundaries. Here, students are learning Tibetan music.

REESTABLISHING THE TIBETAN GOVERNMENT IN EXILE

The Dalai Lama's aptitude for considering the big picture and zeroing in on the critical issues enabled him to make quick decisions and deal with one crisis after another. His natural gift for communicating his vision and inspiring people was instrumental in mobilizing people to rebuild a modern government in exile. Within a few months in exile, he set up the first elected representative body in Tibet's history. He encouraged women to participate in the newly established government by reserving several seats for them. Tibetans who were scattered in refugee camps, road camps and settlements across India and Nepal voted for the first time in their lives. It created a sense of national identity among the diaspora, among people who came from different regions, each with their own dialect, style of clothing, food, and culture. Instead of identifying themselves from Lhasa or one of three provinces—Amdo, Kham, U-Tsang—it unified them as Tibetans. September 2, 1960, continues to be observed as the first anniversary of Democracy Day by the Tibetan diaspora, reinforcing this unity.

The Tibetan community wholly accepted the Central Tibetan Administration (CTA) as the legitimate leadership. Although it is not a legally recognized nation state, India, the non-governmental organizations (NGOs), and other international governments recognize CTA as the representative of the Tibetan diaspora. The CTA consists of an Executive Cabinet with an elected Head (Sikyong) and Ministers, a Judiciary, and a Legislature, and operates as a State within a State. Under the guidance of the Dalai Lama, three key departments were created to administer critical issues facing the diaspora. These were: educating the children, providing housing and employment for the refugees, and preserving Tibetan culture through reestablishing cultural and religious institutions. The Department for Religion & Culture started operations as early as April 1959 to preserve Tibetan religious and cultural heritage. The Department of Home was charged with the settlement and the welfare of the diaspora. Nearly all the refugee concerns are coordinated by the Department of Home, making it possible for the seventy-one settlements and cluster units in India, Nepal, and Bhutan to share experiences and collaborate with each other. The Department of Education was also formed in 1960 to oversee the educational affairs of the Tibetan community, which consists of seventy-three schools, excluding the pre-primary and private schools.

During the fourth anniversary of the Tibetan National Uprising Day in 1963, the Dalai Lama announced he had drafted a constitution for the Tibetan government. It would provide the Tibetans with fundamental human rights preserved in a written constitution. It would, however, take nearly thirty years for its approval. The Dalai Lama explained his impassioned drive to reform the government—even when his people opposed it:

> In 1963, I developed a draft democratic constitution framework. In it, I mentioned that there are circumstances in which the Dalai Lama's power can be abolished by a two-thirds majority. The people disagreed with that part and said it should not be included. I insisted that the clause be left in. Eventually, the Charter of Tibet-in-Exile was adopted in 1991.

The Dalai Lama therefore relinquished his political head-of-state position gradually. The democratization process began in 1990 with the election of the Tibetan Cabinet (Kashag). Previously, the Dalai Lama had appointed the Cabinet. Then, in 2001, Tibetans directly elected the Kalong Tripa. Although Lobsang Tenzin Samdhong Rinpoche was elected Head of CTA, the Dalai Lama continued to preside over the government. The Dalai Lama's long-term aspiration to democratize the Tibetan community was finally fulfilled in 2011. Lobsang Sangay was elected the head of the CTA, and all the Dalai Lama's political authority was transferred to him. His succession was fully realized with his historic feat. Upon his retirement at the age of seventy-six, he succeeded in implementing a democratic government. The Tibetan government in exile is no longer dependent on the leadership of the Dalai Lama. The Tibetan refugees have established the three pillars of democracy—legislature, judiciary, and executive—with the Dalai Lama serving in none of these capacities. In doing so, His Holiness succeeded in establishing a government that will survive him. The Dalai Lama's speech articulates his vision for a democratic government and its fulfillment.

> One of the aspirations I have cherished since childhood is the reform of Tibet's political and social structure, and in the few years that I held effective power in Tibet, I managed to make some fundamental changes. Although I was unable to take this further in Tibet, I have made every effort to do so since we came into

exile. Today, within the framework of the Charter for Tibetans in Exile, the Kalon Tripa, the political leadership, and the people's representatives are directly elected by the people. We have been able to implement democracy in exile that is in keeping with the standards of an open society.

Since I made my intention clear I have received repeated and earnest requests both from within Tibet and outside, to continue to provide political leadership. My desire to devolve authority has nothing to do with a wish to shirk responsibility. It is to benefit Tibetans in the long run. It is not because I feel disheartened. Tibetans have placed such faith and trust in me that as one among them I am committed to playing my part in the just cause of Tibet. I trust that gradually people will come to understand my intention, will support my decision, and accordingly let it take effect.

A leader by birthright, the Dalai Lama had legitimacy. More importantly, he had the love of his people. However, he had no interest in the power and the prestige of ruling; he used his position to serve his country and his people. He was always wary of a government that was reliant on one person. Even before exile he believed in reform and, in exile, has made unprecedented changes.

Gangchen Kyishon, Government compound

Dharamsala

CREATING THE CAPITAL

When I visited Dharamsala in 2014, Nobel Laureates Mairead Maguire, Jody Williams and Shirin Ebadi were speakers at a ceremony to celebrate the 25th anniversary of the Dalai Lama receiving the Nobel Peace Prize. On a later visit, there was a large group of Taiwanese Buddhists, glowing from the teaching they had received from the Dalai Lama. In 2018, when I visited during the Losar (New Year) celebration, Dharamsala was brimming with more Tibetans, who had come from the settlements and the West to celebrate the Tibetan new year and to attend the Dalai Lama's teachings, than there were foreigners.

I didn't expect any more buildings could be squeezed along the hillside, but I was mistaken. In the four years between my last and current visit, new restaurants and upscale hotels had sprung from tiny spaces. Older hotels were renovated to cater to the increasing number of international visitors. I checked in at Pema Thang Guest House where I had previously stayed. It had a small cottage on a patio with a nice panoramic view of the valley. The only drawback was that monkeys used the roof as a shortcut well into the night and early in the morning. The amount of construction reminded me of growing up in Tokyo in the 1950s and 1960s where it was akin to living in a construction site. Internet cafes have also sprouted all over Dharamsala. Instead of reading emails in a dingy shack, we had a choice of going to an Indian, Tibetan, or Western Cafe for cappuccino, espresso or chai tea while catching up on our emails. The obligatory passwords—"Yakyak, Lhasa, Buttertea"—are posted on the tables. There are so many taxis that, at times they seem to be parked rather than being stuck in traffic. It was often faster to walk the mile from the hotel to the Library of Tibetan Works and Archives. When I first arrived in Dharamsala in 2018 after years of absence, I walked around the town looking for familiar signposts. The women selling Tibetan dumplings, *momos*, from their pushcarts were gone as were the shopkeepers sitting outside their stores knitting. However, the women weaving the beautiful Tibetan carpets were still working behind closed doors of the tourist shops. How did this transfiguration into a more modern and bustling town happen?

In part, the transformation can be attributed to the Dalai Lama. In the late sixties, nearly ten years into exile, the Dalai Lama finally relocated to his own cottage where he lived the life of a monk. In contrast to the splendor of the Potala Palace, with its thousand rooms and 10,000 shrines filled with precious relics, treasures, and

7,000 volumes of Buddhist text, the Dalai Lama now possessed almost nothing. His cottage isn't much larger than the temporary one he had shared with his mother; however, it is part of a newly built compound consisting of the Private Office, the Indian Security Office, an office for His Holiness, and an audience room. Outside the audience room is a courtyard filled with potted flowers. Long lines of people stand around this courtyard to await their turn to meet with the Dalai Lama.

The Dalai Lama's personal monastery, which was previously housed in the Potala Palace, was rebuilt within the compound by the fifty-five monks who had escaped with him. When Namgyal Monastery was built, the Dalai Lama stipulated a modest budget in keeping with the refugee situation. He wanted a simple and functional place to offer prayers for the Tibetan refugees and for him to perform Buddhist ceremonies. The monastery supports the Dalai Lama in his religious activities; his personal attendants are drawn from among the monks of the Namgyal Monastery. The monks, in their maroon robes and shaved heads, both symbols of simplicity and detachment from materialism, looked somewhat indistinguishable, though over the weeks, I saw they played different roles within the monastic structure.

The heart and soul of Dharamsala is the Tsuglagkhang Temple, located in the Thekchen Choling complex, outside the gate of the Dalai Lama's compound. Tibetan pilgrims make their way up the stairs, light butter lamps, prostrate, and turn the prayer wheels which line the walls of the courtyard. In one of my visits, I witnessed a small child mimic her parents' praying and making offerings before the Dalai Lama's throne in the temple. She was clumsy, but her parents made no attempt to correct her: they were engrossed in their own prayers. But even if they weren't, they would smile, like I did. In time, they will explain the meaning of the rituals to her.

While the temple attracts hundreds of pilgrims and visitors a year, it is the resident monks that I was drawn to. The first time I witnessed the monks debating, I couldn't grasp the commotion. There was a great deal of elaborate foot stomping, loud clapping, jostling, and yelling. At times, the monks were debating one on one, but other times several monks joined together to debate one monk. The one standing appeared to challenge and the one sitting looked as though he was defending. The one standing did the clapping and stomping. The challenger also used the prayer beads—wrapping them around his arm or holding them behind him. These gestures, I found out later, are highly ritualistic and show specific meaning—the left hand represents wisdom, and the right hand represents method, so the clapping of hands depicts the joining of wisdom and method. These rigorous debates test students' progress in their studies. I thought debates were relegated to monks, but a few days later I observed the nuns debating, causing as much ruckus as the monks and in even higher pitches. Years later, I heard that the Dalai Lama encourages everyone to debate and is delighted to attend elders' debates in the settlements.

A circumambulatory path surrounds the ridge of the Thekchen Choling complex. Buddhist followers can be seen in the early mornings and evenings walking clockwise, stopping from time to time to pay respect to religious objects found along the path. Nearby, there is the Home for Old Men and Women. One hundred and fifty people over the age of sixty live there. For the Tibetans, as in many other Asian cultures, it's traditional for people of different generations to live under the same roof. Those who live in the senior homes do not have families. Most of the rooms are for two people; however, there are a few single rooms reserved for monks, nuns, and those who practice Buddhism throughout the day. I was told there are thirteen homes in various settlements, but this one has the longest waiting

The Dalai Lama greeting Tibetan visitors in the courtyard of his compound.

list. Even though they may not see the Dalai Lama very often, knowing he lives nearby gives them comfort. In the afternoons, the residents who can walk attend the prayer sessions with resident monks and nuns leading the prayers and chanting.

My itinerary was so tightly packed I had to keep to my schedule; however, one relatively appointment-free day, Dorje Gyaltsen, the representative from the Home Office, brought me to visit the hermits who live high up the mountain ridge. When the doors to their caves are shut, it indicates they are meditating. We climbed higher up the steep slope until a friendly monk, who was on his lunch break, invited us in. He had escaped from Tibet nearly twenty years ago. After studying in one of the large monasteries in southern India, he decided that he wanted to be a hermit. He has lived in his cave for about eight years, leaving only to attend the Dalai Lama's teachings. I had placed money in an envelope as an offering but felt rather ridiculous because I realized that he had no need for money, but would have welcomed tea and sugar, which Dorje brought. We met another hermit who had been there for over twenty years. Over time, people had brought him paint for his walls and carpet for his floor. He said that he stopped attending teachings: he stays in his cave and chants. A third monk was an elderly

Pilgrims and visitors spinning prayer wheels in the Tsuglagkhang Temple courtyard.

These novice monks look like they are bantering, but they are engaged in a philosophical debate.

man with a deeply lined face. He said when he was young, he hated the Chinese so much he joined the military so he could kill them. When he realized the Chinese people weren't to blame, he became a monk and has devoted himself to the practice of Buddhism. He said he no longer hates the Chinese. When we visited another monk, Dorje became guarded. I had only seen him as a warm and friendly person, so I knew something didn't sit well with him. We left the hermit quickly and I noticed Dorje did not leave him any of the tea he had brought. Dorje said he frequently brings food and tea to the hermits but had never seen this monk; he suspected that the person had donned a monk's robe in hopes of collecting offerings. I learned there are rotten apples in every culture, yet he was the only one I met in my years of travels among the Tibetans.

About a mile downhill from the Dalai Lama's compound is the Gangchen Kyishong. The CTA, its departments, and the Prime Minister's residence is in this compound. The Library of Tibetan Works and Archives (LTWA) is considered one of the most important libraries and institutions of its kind. It was built in 1970 to protect, preserve, restore, and promote Tibetan culture. The library houses invaluable Buddhist manuscripts and artifacts which were carried by the Tibetans as they escaped and later given to the Dalai Lama. Its resources include more than 80,000 manuscripts, books, and documents, over 600 thangka paintings, statues, and other Buddhist artifacts and 6,000 photographs related to Tibet's history, culture, and art. A museum is located on the third floor of the library. Some of the artifacts date to the twelfth century, reflecting the lives and culture of the Tibetan people. In the museum, they can see their cultural tradition and take pride in their distinct heritage. One Tibetan woman said her parents burst into tears when she took them to the third-floor museum. For the Tibetans, who have been chanting Buddhist mantras or prayers, while visualizing deities their entire life, the

artifacts represent what is in their mind's eyes. Seeing their ancient artwork preserved for centuries not only touches them emotionally but gives them the hope that their culture will live on.

When I visited the library in 2009, there was scaffolding around the entrance. Two monks, trained in sacred art, were painting elaborate Buddhist murals on the ceiling. In the reading room, a librarian was carefully folding yellow cloth over the long rectangular manuscripts, then labeling them. These manuscripts are a replica of the original Buddhist manuscripts written on palm paper. In my last visit to Dharamsala, the Library had added another story by enclosing the roof terrace. The library has undertaken additional responsibilities, including the translation of several works from Tibetan into English. The library also attracts large numbers of international scholars, students, and visitors interested in Buddhist and Tibetan studies. Buddhist philosophy and the Tibetan language are taught in the adjacent building. Geshe Lhakdor, LTWA's Director, is tasked by the Dalai Lama to integrate modern science into the curriculum of monastic education. On the first floor, English and Tibetan books that are published by the library are sold.

Men-Tsee-Khang, the Tibetan Medical and Astrological Institute, is located further down the hill in its own compound. It was established to preserve, promote, and practice the ancient Tibetan system of medicine, astronomy, and astrology. In addition to providing healthcare to the diaspora and producing traditional medicine, the institute engages in research and higher education. Tibetan medicine is produced on the premise of using a combination of manual labor and modern equipment. The workers pound stones to harvest minerals, and grind roots and bark from plants and trees. The powder is mixed and formed into small round balls. These are dried on sheets on the roof of the institute. The Dalai Lama indicated that Tibetan medical practices are starting to be recognized in India. He thinks there is potential for Tibetan medical practices to be recognized globally. During my visit, there were already many Westerners waiting to see the Tibetan doctors. Some had already had their pulse diagnosed and were waiting for the pharmacists to package large amounts of herbal medicine for them to take back home. They could re-order online and the herbal medicine would be shipped to them.

I visited the Refugee Reception Center, located in the center of Dharamsala, which was crowded with about thirty new refugees. I had noticed them earlier at Tsuglagkhang Temple because, unlike of the serene faces of the Tibetans, theirs appeared listless, and their eyes looked tired and afraid. I couldn't believe I was seeing the same people. After their audience with the Dalai Lama, something had shifted in them—they looked less distraught. No doubt the Dalai Lama had given them a glimpse of a brighter path forward out of the darkness they had come from. The Dalai Lama understands that it is difficult to transition from Tibet to the modern world and has a plan to help them. They were waiting to hear where they would be sent. Monks and nuns were assigned to monasteries, and young children were sent to the TCV. High school graduates were sent to vocational schools to acquire a trade. The Dalai Lama has made sure all new refugees are given support in their new lives and the start of a new journey.

The center had two large rooms—one for women and children, and a second for men. A few of the young men in their early twenties were in the men's dormitory. One of them approached me and asked if I spoke Chinese. When I nodded, he said around the time of the 2008 Beijing Olympics Games, Chinese soldiers came to his room in the middle of the night, grabbed his photograph of the Dalai Lama from the wall and threw him in jail. The next day, they sent him home, but kept his identity papers. His grandfather had told him not to keep any photographs of the Dalai Lama, but he had thought his grandfather was being overly cautious. When his grandfather heard what had happened, he was certain the Chinese police would come back and lock up his grandson for good. The young man and a few of his friends escaped the next evening. As I listened, I tried to stay composed, trying not to show that my stomach was churning from the story of their ordeal. Much of what he said was in a whisper and at times he spoke fast without pausing. I could tell he was reliving the frightening experience. All I could do was to appear calm and listen with unconditional compassion. When he finished, he thanked me for listening and said he felt much better after telling his story. I have been an executive coach for many years and believe in the power of listening. But never have I witnessed such a dramatic transformation—from fear to relief and from holding on to letting go. It was as though all the grime from his grueling escape had been dusted off as he recounted his story. From this experience, I realized the power of *nying je chenmo*, or great compassion, an advanced state of spiritual development which Buddhist practitioners try to attain, and the Dalai Lama possesses in abundance. I began to see the Dalai Lama's power of compassion. He is a good listener because he has enhanced sensitivity towards other people's suffering and genuinely wants to help them overcome their suffering. This group of refugees is referred to as the third wave. The first wave followed the Dalai Lama into exile in 1959, the second wave occurred in the 1980s when China partially opened Tibet to foreign travelers, and the third wave began in the late 1990s. In recent years, it's been nearly impossible to escape from Tibet: the number of Tibetan refugees has dwindled to almost none.

Hermit meditating in his cave.

Tibetan woman spinning her prayer wheel, which is filled with written mantras, or prayers. As she chants, she is releasing blessings into the world. Tibetans believe that when spoken blessings are repeated, they accumulate like rain clouds.

REBUILDING COMMUNITIES

If the Tibetan refugees had their wish, they would all be living in Dharamsala near their treasured leader. In fact, there are more Tibetans living in Dharamsala than in any of the settlements. The altitude of Dharamsala is closer to what they are used to, and Tibet is just out of reach on the other side of the distant mountain ranges. But because so many Tibetans followed the Dalai Lama into exile, living near him was impossible. Fearing the loss of Tibetan culture should the refugees be scattered in different directions, the Dalai Lama and Pandit Nehru developed settlements for the refugees. When the southern Indian state of Karnataka offered 3,000 acres of jungle—an acre per person—for the development of autonomous settlements, the Dalai Lama gratefully accepted. The Dalai Lama first visited Bylakuppe in the early 1960s just as the refugees were clearing the jungle, digging wells, building houses, and cultivating the land. They were reluctant to plant fruit trees because they believed they would return to Tibet before the trees bore fruit. It could not have been very easy for the Dalai Lama to discover that many of the refugees had died from sunstroke and heat exhaustion. In his autobiography, the Dalai Lama questioned if he had been right in accepting land in the tropics. Although uncertain himself, he encouraged them to persevere, telling them that the future of Tibet itself depended on the refugees building strong communities. Having a common experience with his people, he understood exactly how they felt but didn't let them wallow in their sorrow. He said he had faith in them just as they had faith in him:

> *Often, I had to console the refugees in their sadness when I visited these camps. The thought of being so far from home and with no prospect of seeing ice or snow, let alone our beloved mountains, was hard for them to bear. I tried to take their minds off the past. Instead, I told them that the future of Tibet depended on us refugees. If we wanted to preserve our culture and way of life, the only way to do so was by building strong communities.*

The Dalai Lama was still in his mid-twenties when he was confronted with the tremendous task of leading and guiding his people in a foreign land after the devastating loss of their country and freedom. The route he chose led the

Tibetans to freedom, if not of country, of spirit. How did he manage it? The Dalai Lama did not micro-manage the resettlement of the Tibetan diaspora. Thupten Jinpa, the Dalai Lama's principal English translator since 1985, who has read the Dalai Lama' personal notes taken during those years, said this period was a very important spiritual and formative time for the Dalai Lama. As he delved deeper into his own spiritual practice and training, his focus was on two major themes: "cultivation of compassion, universal compassion, and deepening his understanding of the view of emptiness and interdependent reality." Thupten Jinpa added, "I think it was a very contemplative, reflective period for him. And he often speaks about how those ten years were really formative in his own spiritual, personal, and meditative development and cultivation."[2]

Most of the settlements were constructed between 1960 and 1965, freeing the refugees from roadwork. Clearing the jungle and building the settlements was not as hazardous as roadwork; nonetheless, it had its challenges. The average elevation in Tibet is 14,750 feet (4,500 meters) compared with that of Southern India at 3,360 feet (1,024 meters). The Tibetan farmers employed a highly efficient irrigation and water distribution process built around melting snow. This knowledge was futile in southern India, where farmers rely on rain from the monsoon season for irrigation.

I visited all five settlements in Karnataka in 2009. To reach Bylakuppe, I flew into Bengaluru Airport, then was driven 160 miles. For those who have visited India, it would not seem surprising that this short distance took six hours. Drivers don't always stay within their lane but weave in and out to avoid hitting cows and people crossing the street wherever and whenever they want. There is always a cacophony of honking. Outside of cities, long wheat stalks are bunched and placed on the road for cars to drive over. Indian women in saris could be seen squatting on the road with baskets by their sides, picking the heads of the wheat.

Entrances to the Tibetan settlements are usually marked with undistinguished signs. However, upon setting foot in the settlements, it is unmistakable—you are not in India anymore. Rows of prayer flags, when windy, are blowing in the wind. All the settlements have premises for the settlement officers and their staff, community halls, dispensaries, homes for seniors, residential houses, and schools. Monasteries and nunneries are situated on the edge of the settlements. Each of the settlements has its own unique characteristics largely due to its location. Besides the five settlements in Southern India, there are settlements within a day's drive from Dharamsala as well as settlements further north in Ladakh, with smaller settlements scattered in Eastern India and in Sikkim and Nepal.

The settlements are managed according to a formal organizational structure, its leaders have clearly defined roles and responsibilities. The settlement officers, who are employed by the Department of Home, develop policies, identify, and plan projects with their staff, oversee the settlements with the help of camp leaders, and interact with the local Indian communities. The larger settlements accommodate from 1,000–8,000 refugees. Too large for one person to manage, they are further divided into camps headed by camp leaders, and, in some cases, even with assistant camp leaders. The two first settlements—Lugsung Samdupling, founded in 1961 and Dekyi Larsoe, founded in 1969—are large and have many assistant camp leaders who are responsible for the execution of project plans. Each of the settlements manages its own cooperative which owns tractors and warehouses to store grain. The cooperatives purchase seeds, sell surplus food, and run animal husbandry centers and machine repair shops. Although initially owned and managed by CTA, the exiled government, these cooperatives were turned over to the local communities to develop managerial skills. Those in charge of the cooperatives enthusiastically explained their new responsibilities to me, but were quick to add, "due to the vision of His Holiness, we have our own cooperatives," or "we started organic farming" and so forth. What impressed me was their devotion to the Dalai Lama. He is their beloved leader, and the Tibetans attribute their own successes to him. Successful organizations require good leaders, but they also need good followership. Their mutual trust—the people's trust in him to guide them, and his trust in them to adapt to life in exile—has resulted in establishing strong settlement communities. By transferring ownership and responsibility from the central government to the settlements, the refugees are acquiring invaluable managerial skills.

On my first visit to Bylakuppe, in 2009, large groups of Tibetans were sitting outside the community center chanting prayers. During tea breaks, women poured tea and served butter cookies. If these prayers didn't bring the much-needed rain, the next step would be to go into the fields chanting prayers. Fortunately, the monsoon did come, and the harvest was saved. Settlement officers were more than happy to show me around; in fact, they crammed so much into my day, I am hard pressed to remember the places I visited and the people I met. What I remember best about Bylakuppe is a fifty-eight-year-old woman who was looking after her bedridden parents. Her grace, serenity, and compassion radiated around her. In comparison with the other houses in the settlement, hers was sparse. The few things she owned were simple and utilitarian.

What I remember was how everything was placed attentively as if they were precious offerings for the altar. Even the baskets she used to gather fruits and vegetables, firewood, and dried barley were carefully placed by the entrance of her immaculate cottage. She had mango, coconut, banana, guava, and apple trees and had planted beans, eggplants, and lots of green vegetables in her small kitchen garden. Because she is looking after her bedridden elder parents and unable to work, the settlement provides her with a small stipend. In this way, elder parents can be cared for by their own children. Her only child is attending university.

Later that day, I wandered around alone. A friendly middle-aged woman invited me to see her house. She didn't speak English or Chinese, so we used hand gestures. In her barn she had a cow and a calf. I didn't quite realize how important her cow was until she pointed out her roof terrace, which had prayer flags on all four sides. I had thought she was drying fruits, but when I climbed up the ladder, to my surprise her terrace was filled with patties of cow dung. Shocked, I looked down only to see her happy smile.

In nearby Hunsur, the settlement officer of this small settlement told me when the refugees first came here, they would let their cows wander freely, but found their livestock would disappear in the jungle. They concluded there must have been tigers. At the time that I visited, the biggest challenge for them was the elephants. They had dug a deep ditch around their farmland, but, regardless of how deep, the highly intelligent elephants have been able to get to the harvest just as it ripened. Tibetans treat the lives of all living beings with respect, so whether it's elephants eating their harvest, or monkeys at another settlement eating their bananas, they will not harm the animals.

Dhondenling in Kollegal, the fourth settlement in the south, is picturesque, with uniform cottages painted in white. The monasteries, which are brightly adorned with prayer flags, rise high above the settlement, perched at the edge of the surrounding mountains. Gazing out at the harmonious landscape of nature and architecture, I wondered if villages in Tibet looked like this. It was obvious the residents took care of their homes. It was the tenth day of the Tibetan calendar, a special Buddhist day. The residents were attending prayers in the makeshift monastery while the actual monastery was being renovated. Each Wednesday, the villagers go to the Dalai Lama's palace to pray for his long life. Karma Singay, the settlement officer, took special interest in the seniors who live in the community elder homes. He told me that Tibetans care for their own elder parents, so these seniors are the ones without children to look after them. The seniors live in a single-story compound surrounding a beautiful courtyard full of flowers. When we arrived, they were sitting in the courtyard, silently chanting mantras and counting them on their mala beads. When they spotted Karma Singay, they came alive. I photographed them together and then individually and printed them for Karma Singay to hang in his office. They loved his visits and hated to see him go, even if they knew he would be back in a few days.

The fifth settlement in southern India, Doeguling Settlement in Mundgod, is a large settlement with 17,000 residents and four large monasteries with around 8,000 monks and nuns living in them. I was staying at the settlement's guest house, which used to be one wing of the Dalai Lama's monastery. It had a lovely porch, but it was monsoon season, rampant with mosquitoes, so I went indoors, hoping the screen would keep them out. Palden Dhondup, the head of the settlement, picked me up to have a breakfast of Tibetan tea and bread. Afterwards, we went to Drepung Loseling, one of the three large teaching monasteries in Lhasa, which had been rebuilt by the 250 monks who fled to India in 1959. The monastery is dedicated to the study and preservation of the Tibetan Buddhist tradition of wisdom and compassion. After completing a twenty-year course of intense study and training, and an examination, students qualify for the Geshe Lharampa degree. The seventh Kyabje Yongzin Ling Rinpoche, the reincarnation of Dalai Lama's principal tutor (the sixth reincarnation 1903–1983), had enrolled in Drepung Monastery University's Loseling College in 1990 and was studying for his Geshe degree under the guidance of the Dalai Lama.

I happened to go to the daycare center as the children were having lunch. Even at that young age, children are taught responsibilities and to be self-sufficient. After collecting aluminum pots filled with rice, dahl, and vegetables from the kitchen, children served their classmates who were sitting on the school's cement floor, hungrily waiting for their lunch. After our lunch, I met Rinzin Wangmo, the settlement secretary, who had just graduated from TCV. She said because so much of the correspondence is in Tibetan, one must have Tibetan language proficiency in order to work for the Home Office. She took me to the community hospital and the TB ward behind the hospital. We put on masks and went in. There is still a high rate of TB in the settlements and in the monasteries due to the proximity of their living quarters.

It was an unusually busy week for the settlement: a "Thank you India" celebration, a birthday celebration for the Dalai Lama, and a Long-Life Prayer for him. I was left on my own to wander around the settlement for a few hours.

Tibetan woman in her one-room home. The Tibetans serve tea as part of their hospitality. The brown churn is used to make butter tea, traditionally made with tea leaves, yak butter, and salt.

Tuk-tuks (motorized versions of the cycled rickshaw), motorcycles, cars, and water buffalos compete for the right of way on muddy roads. The buffaloes, nicknamed "king of the road," always win. In the afternoon, Tibetans and local Indian students competed in a soccer match. It appeared as if the whole settlement— monastic and lay—attended. Though the field was muddy from days of rain, the sun had come out. The settlement officer was very nervous about the relationship between the local Indians and the Tibetans: judging from the crowd of locals and refugees, he didn't need to worry. Playing sports can really build strong relationships.

The following day, on the Dalai Lama's birthday, we climbed a steep hill to find that early risers had already piled the stupa with dozens of long white kata scarves as a sign of respect for the Dalai Lama. Everyone was dressed in traditional Tibetan clothing. A special flavored rice was offered to the monks,

who were praying for the Dalai Lama's long life. At the conclusion of the ceremony, the Tibetans stood up in a big semi-circle and threw powdered barley in the air, a gesture of celebration and joy. I wasn't fast enough to cover my camera: it took a lot of cleaning to get the powder off the lens. We then headed downhill to the community center where speeches—a lot of them—were given in turn by the Abbot and Tibetan and Indian government officials. After lunch, we went to the monastery where students attended Ling Rinpoche's teaching.

In the first decade following the diaspora, the Indian Government continued to accept Tibetan refugees seeking asylum and leased them land in various regions throughout India. Although the settlements were designed as self-contained agricultural units serving the needs of first and second-generation refugees, since not all the refugees were farmers, agro-industrial and handicraft-based settlements were also developed to accommodate the traders, craftspeople, and nomads who had little knowledge of farming. Experiments with small-scale industries, such as growing tea, were also tried with various degrees of success.

Bir is situated in the foothills of the Himalayas in the state of Himachal Pradesh in north India. This small Tibetan settlement is a two-and-a-half-hour drive by car from Dharamsala through winding tea gardens. I was happy to meet a female settlement officer. She took me to a monastery bustling with both lay and monastic people making prayer wheels. Prayers are printed on rolled paper which are carefully trimmed and placed into spools, which are then covered by a brass cylinder. I was just in time for tea. People stopped their work and had tea and butter cookies. Coming from two tea cultures, I was grateful to be included. There are also several institutions in and around Bir. Deer Park Institute, a center for the study of classic Indian wisdom traditions, was established by Dzongsar Khyentse Rinpoche in 2006 under the patronage of the Dalai Lama. The Dzongsar Khyentse Chokyi Lodro Institute is in nearby Chauntra.

There are also several settlements in East India. Kunphenling is a small settlement in Ravangla, a hill station situated at an elevation of 8,000 feet in the State of Sikkim in Northeast India, bordered by Bhutan, China, Tibet, and Nepal. Sikkim, once an independent nation, was incorporated into India in 1975. In October, after a heavy rainstorm, the road from Kalimpong was nearly impassable due to landslides, giant potholes, and fallen trees and wires. The sun peeked through thick clouds and revealed a lush settlement. I learned, however, that looks can be deceiving —the land is impoverished. It rains six

Throwing barley to celebrate the Dalai Lama's birthday.

months out of the year, and when it is not raining, it is foggy. The Tibetans cover their ceilings with thick plastic sheets to prevent the fog from rolling into their homes.

Jampa Nobling picked me up at eight to take me to the school his son was attending. Unlike many of the men who joined the Indian Army, Jampa Nobling and his wife weave carpets. Their three daughters attend TCV in Dharamsala, but their young son lives with them. They plan to emigrate to Canada for the sake of their four children. The children were lined up, did some stretching, then folded their palms together and prayed. At the same time, the sun shone through masses of billowing clouds, revealing hidden mountain peaks. The photograph of the children in their uniform—navy blue sweaters and skirts for girls and slacks for boys—apart from a young boy, who didn't have a sponsor to buy him a uniform, praying earnestly and standing with their teachers dressed in Tibetan *chupas* is one of my favorite photographs. The Dalai Lama has said the future of Tibet depends on the children. I felt certain every child there would grow up steeped in Tibetan culture as well as the principles of being a compassionate human being.

Tibetan children begin the day praying for loving kindness and peace to all.

IN SEARCH OF NOMADS

The Tibetan diaspora adapted their way of life to live in a low altitude country in all the settlements in India, with the exception of those living in Ladakh. This settlement is located on the outskirts of Leh, the capital of Ladakh, at 11,483 feet (3,524 meters) which is only 500 feet lower in altitude than Lhasa at 11,995 feet. Many of the Tibetan nomads settled in Sonamling Settlement, located in the high plateau of the Himalayas in the state of Jammu and Kashmir. Although they were nomads in Tibet, the majority now worked in Leh as traders, small cafe and shop owners, construction workers, and tenders of animals for trekking. There are, however, 1,539 nomads living in tents at 17,000 feet (5,300 meters). They subsist as herders, following their yak, dzo (a hybrid between the yak and domestic cattle), sheep, and goats from summer to winter pastures. The remoteness of the place and vanishing lifestyle only added to my desire to get a first-hand look at their nomadic lifestyle. I asked Tashi, a Ladakhi driver and one of the few local children to attend the Tibetan Children's Village School, to drive me. We set off early in the morning to beat the local traffic. It took two days of driving through spectacular mountain landscapes on narrow mountain paths to get to Thadsang Karu Lake, where the nomads were camped for the summer.

At over 17,000 feet (5,300 meters), there is no vegetation. The already thin air felt even thinner. The towering, snowcapped Himalayas silhouetted against the vibrant blue sky and the exhilarating sense of openness was breathtaking. Just a month ago, this road was covered by snow and impassable. Today, there was still ice on the road and icicles along the side of the road. Spotting a tent, I got out of the car. As I approached, a dog barked and then lunged at me. I had read those Tibetan mastiffs were used by nomads to protect sheep from wolves, leopards, bears, and tigers, but was little prepared for how vicious and large they are. I sprung back and ran as fast as I could, although I could hardly breathe and my chest felt tight in the thin air. Tashi drove his 4-wheeler between me and the growling dog. I leapt in. Only then did I see the dog was tied to a post by the tent. Two small children poked out their heads from inside—the dog was protecting the children from strangers!

We drove what seemed like miles until we came to another tent. A toothless woman appeared from the small tent and thrust something in my face. "Very old," she said, and beckoned me to enter her tent where she had many more items

laid on a filthy cloth. I couldn't make out what these things were and must have looked as if I was interested. "Antique," she said. Shaking my head, I got back into the car. We drove further up the mountain.

At a third tent, a young mother smiled and held open the flap for me to enter. Inside, her infant son was bundled in a wool blanket and cradled in yak fur. He smiled and gurgled. His three brothers, a year to two years apart, first stared, then tried to grab my attention by making faces and the ubiquitous peace sign. Tashi came to get me, saying we were invited to stay with the family living in the nearby tent. What a comfortable and large tent it was. The canvas was woven from yak hair and the ground was covered with canvas and well-worn woolen Tibetan carpets the size of a single bed. We instinctively took off our hiking boots as we entered.

Tenzin Sangmo, a young woman in her early twenties, poured us butter-tea. Fortunately, the milk was from goats and not yak, which would have been much stronger. She then proceeded to knead dough, which she covered and placed aside. There were two stoves, one in the middle of the tent with a chimney thrust out to an opening in the center of the tent and a second, smaller one, placed near the entrance. She then washed the rice, and placed the pot on the larger stove, washed the lentils, placed it on the smaller stove, and tipped the water into a bowl outside the tent. When the dough had doubled in size, she rolled the dough into a long snake shape, cut it into one-inch pieces, then rolled each one into a small bun. The buns were placed in a steamer on top of the pot holding the rice. She then peeled and chopped potatoes and dropped them in a covered pan. Now and then she threw a handful of dried goat dung into the fire—it was surprisingly odorless.

I was so absorbed with the rhythmic ease in which Tenzin Sangmo prepared the meal, it was not until she finished that I looked around the tent. There were half a dozen rolled up blankets along the side of the tent. At the back, facing the entrance, was an altar with seven silver bowls filled with water, an incense holder, and Buddhist statues. On a low table there was a radio, nail polish, and makeup. I was puzzled why a nomadic woman would use makeup, but before I could ask her, a cacophony of yells, whistles, bleating, and crying in shotgun cadence pierced the quiet. I pulled my boots on and dashed outside. Hundreds of *changthangi* (pashmina or cashmere) goats with long white fur glistened in the evening sun. These rare goats, found in Ladakh and Kashmir, are raised for their fine, soft downy winter undercoats, which grow as the days shorten. Tenzin Sangmo's father told me that it takes the fine wool of three goats to make a pashmina shawl. In the distance, three men on horseback were shouting and whistling to the lagging goats, rounding them up closer to the tent. A middle-aged woman herded the goats on foot. At six o'clock, it was already very cold. By evening, the temperature would drop below freezing.

   After the goats were cared for, the men came inside the tent for butter-tea and conversation. Tashi's English was too poor to translate, but I imagined they were reflecting on the day. Tashi said that most of the nomads had started to trek farther up the mountain, as food for the herds was dwindling. The yaks had already climbed higher into the Himalayas in search of grass, shrubs, and cooler temperature. I had read that yak do not eat grain and will starve unless they have grass to eat. Their physiology was adapted to high altitude: their particularly large lungs and hearts are unsuited to lower altitudes. In fact, they suffer from heat exhaustion when the temperature rises above 59 degrees Fahrenheit. Earlier, we had seen a family head up the mountain with their belongings neatly piled on two horses. Tenzin Sangmo's large extended family would need a truck.

   Tenzin Sangmo's parents, both in their fifties, were born in Tibet. She and her five brothers were born in Ladakh. Her oldest brother, also a nomad, lives in the nearby tent with his wife and three boys. The second elder brother is a monk in Sikkim, the third is employed by the Indian army, and the two younger brothers are both attending the TCV. She herself graduated from TCV and works in a town. They were all home helping their parents during their summer holiday. Even though this diversity may seem unusual to non-Tibetans, this configuration is common among the nomadic population in exile.

   After a lively dinner, the family members each withdrew into their personal space in the tent: Sangmo recited *mantras*, or prayers, at the altar; her father spun his prayer wheel and softly recited mantras; her mother sat in silence, no doubt reciting a mantra, as she braided long ropes. Sangmo's teenage brother was helping their younger brother with an English essay. It was only then that I discovered they spoke English. "I am a nomad boy," he read from his essay, "and I helped my parents herd goats during the school holiday…" I asked the teenager if he would follow his father's footsteps when he graduated. With a big smile, he said, "No, being a nomad is too hard. I am going to go into commerce."

   I had the choice of spending the night in the large tent with the family or in the smaller tent packed with dry *chhurpi* (Tibetan cheese made with yak milk) and yak hide. I opted to sleep in the car. Tashi chose the small tent. He later told me a few goats wandered in during the night. At least they kept him warm.

I had a terrible night—the back seat of the 4-wheeler was cramped, and I had a throbbing headache from the high altitude. I finally fell asleep but was soon jolted awake. What noise! The goats were rubbing themselves against the car and bleating. Looking out the window, I was transported to a cinema screening of a documentary on Tibetan nomads. The purple blue morning light cast an enchanted glow, against which puffy clouds, snowcapped mountains, and barren earth formed the backdrop. Scene one: Tenzin Sangmo, her mother, her sister-in-law, and her teenage brother herd the goats, brandishing the rope woven the previous evening. They move effortlessly in coordinated fashion like a seasoned sports team. The lactating goats are tied—head-to-head—in two rows. Her mother and sister-in-law squat and milk the goats. Scene two: The toddler, who is tied to a rock so he doesn't wander off and get trampled by the goats, sucks milk from a bottle. Sangmo's eldest brother absentmindedly peruses the landscape. Then the elder brother does something sweet. He notices his infant son—who is wearing slacks with an open slit down the back—had defecated. He plucks a handful of the fine, soft coat that's scattered atop the coarser outer coat of the

goats and uses it to wipes his son's bottom. Scene three: The men get up on their horses and herd the goats up the mountain.

This was the family's last night at this campsite. Tomorrow, a large truck will take the two families' belongings to a new campsite further up the mountain. Sangmo will go back to work, and her two younger brothers will go back to school. The parents will stay up in the mountains until the winter months and then come down to their winter pasture, further down the mountain.

No doubt the snow intensifies the beauty; however, in the severe winter months when the temperature can drop to -40°F, the reality of nomadic life is harsh and tenuous. In years of extreme cold, they have lost thousands of their livestock to deep snow. In the summer months, when the temperature can get as high as 90°F, the nomads migrate higher and higher in search of grass for their livestock. Such nomadic communities were once cut off from the world, except to trade salt, cheese, and wool, but today their children are attending schools in Leh where they learn from other Tibetans who live in places not steeped in tradition. Through them, these children discover that they have alternatives to

These nomads live in tents all year long. As the yaks move up higher up the Himalayas during the summer months and down during the winter, the nomads fold up their tent and belongings and follow.

being nomads and have the freedom to choose their future. I wondered how much longer this timeless itinerant existence would continue. I also wondered how the Dalai Lama felt about the vanishing nomadic lifestyle. The Dalai Lama is not nostalgic about the Tibet he had known in his youth. He is practical and pragmatic. He is open to new ideas and to modernization. He is willing to face forward and help modernize Tibetan culture and to train his people to fit in with the new world.

"Can the nomadic lifestyle survive?" I asked nomad Tashi Dolma, whom I met in Oakland, California. Tashi Dolma's parents and her three older siblings fled from Rutok in Ngari Prefecture, Tibet to Ladakh in 1961. She is the seventh of eleven children. As the children became of school age, they were sent to Leh to attend the TCV. Tashi said it was so cold in the winter months when the school had two months off, that she would often stay in Leh instead of going home to live in the family tent. After training as a dental assistant, she was assigned as a dentist to the nomads. She lived in a tent for three years, moving with the nomads from summer to winter pastures. She would ride on her horse with two boxes—one for her tools and one for medicine. In the winter months her hands would be so frozen she couldn't move them. There was no heat in the tent. During the summer she got water from the streams, but in the winter, she had to melt ice. Only three of Tashi's siblings are nomads, and only one of their children is a nomad. Speaking about her nomadic siblings, she said, "It is a very hard life, and they are poor. They only have pashmina goat hair to sell to buy barley." Then she added with a faraway smile, "But it is a very peaceful life. The taste of summer yogurt made from fresh milk is unbelievably delicious: you can taste the grass the goats ate."

SWEATER SELLERS

Most Tibetans living in settlements in India supplement their income by selling sweaters in the winter months, from October through February. They return home to the settlement in time for Tibetan New Year and to help with the planting. Sweater stalls are set up around bus and train terminals. In the early days, the sweaters were hand knitted by Tibetans; however, due to their high demand, they are now machine-made in Indian factories. The sweater sellers are also organized in communities with elected officers. When I visited some sweater sellers in Bangalore, I was taken to see the head of the sweater traders. Here, as well, the chain of command is respected. He showed me the storage unit where the makeshift stalls and sweaters are stored overnight as they are not allowed to set up permanent stalls. A Tibetan high school student invited us into a rented temporary apartment. She told us she was visiting her two older sisters during a school break. Her sister, who was asleep on the floor and whom I nearly tripped over, worked the night shift in a call center. A second sister sold sweaters in the stalls. She pulled aside a large sheet to reveal stacks of sweaters from floor to ceiling. Her aging parents, she said, live in one of the settlements.

Children performing a traditional dance during Losar, New Year celebration. Above the Dalai Lama's portrait is a thangka painting of Avalokiteshvara, the bodhisattva of compassion.

A DECADE LATER

When I visited the settlements in southern India forty some years after they were founded, it was apparent that the Tibetans have been able to preserve their culture. While non-Tibetans are allowed to visit during the day, they must obtain a permit from the Indian Government to spend even one night there. The Tibetans living in these settlements speak their own language, practice their own religion, attend their own schools, go to their own clinics, and celebrate their own tradition in isolation from the host country. Most of the older Tibetans only speak Tibetan.

Ten years after my first visit, I was invited by a Tibetan family to spend Losar with them in Bylakuppe. Since the day before Losar is a day to clean the house, they wanted me to stay with them after they had thoroughly cleaned the house. I was dropped off at a nearby monastery's guesthouse, but the monastery was deserted, and the cafe was closed. Monks also return to their families or go to Dharamsala where Losar is celebrated with many special teachings. I was grateful they took me into their home after one night at the guesthouse as I was totally dislocated. The change was astonishing. We remember places we have visited and expect them to remain the same when we revisit, but of course, things change. Most, if not all the houses were rebuilt—mostly from funds sent to them by children who have subsequently emigrated to the West. Some of the more modest homes were rebuilt by the families themselves with help from their children who still live in the settlement. Kelsang Phuntsok Jungney, who has emigrated to the United States, told me that his parents kept patching the original house until it became more economical to tear down the old structure and rebuild. His mother, however, insisted they keep the original house to remind them of their humble past. The original house had two small rooms; the family slept in one and cooked and ate in the other. These houses had no bathrooms, and the floor was made of packed dirt. I was blown away by the transformation. Their new house has a prayer room, a living/dining room, a kitchen at the back of the house, bedrooms, and a bathroom and laundry room. There is electricity and running hot and cold water and even an internet connection. The family rented the empty lot next to their house to grow vegetables. Jigme Jungney said, with a big smile, he and his wife live on vegetables and fruit grown in their own garden.

The settlement came alive during the week-long Losar celebrations. Those Tibetans who sell sweaters outside the settlements had returned home, as had many relatives who had emigrated to the west. Growing up in Japan, I remember the house cleaning before the New Year, and then the endless visits to relatives and friends over the course of many days. Tibetans appeared to have a similar tradition. When assigning the refugees to settlements, an attempt was made to keep extended families in the same settlements. Both Jigme Jungney and his wife Sonam Paldon come from large families, so there were a lot of comings and goings among the extended family. On day one of Losar, the immediate families gather to celebrate the occasion with a special meal (cooked over the previous days). No one does any housework or cooking during New Year's Day. Then people from the same camps celebrate with prayers, music, and dance. Finally, the entire settlement gets together in their large community center to offer prayers and to celebrate Losar with more music and dance.

This time, a wedding celebration of a family member added to the bustle. Huge tents were pitched in the large garden. Two days before the wedding, as was their custom, people from another camp came to stuff sausages, cut up vegetables, knead dough for bread, and decorate the tents. On the day of the wedding, the bride and groom, who were dressed in layers of traditional clothes, sat with their immediate family members in their reception room. As guests entered, they bowed to the family altar, then to the bride and groom, and offered *kata*, a white silk scarf with an envelope carefully tucked into it. They then greeted each family member seated in the reception room. As they left the room, they were escorted to the table where the wedding feast would take place. I noticed here—as I had in other celebratory occasions—Tibetan men, women, and children sit among themselves and do not mingle.

In my earlier visits to the settlements, I had the impression that the settlements would not last. I had only seen elderly people, and on a few occasions, mothers with toddlers, in the settlements. Few of the settlements had newly built homes, so they seemed out of place. In one of the settlements in northern India, there was a power outage during the three days I stayed there. The residents told me they hadn't had electricity for over a week. A cook, however, effortlessly made a delicious meal by candlelight, giving me the impression he had done this many times. However, when I visited in 2018, every house had been rebuilt and modernized. The residents told me it was out of necessity as the original houses were built in the sixties and needed constant repair. In the end it was cheaper to tear down the old structures, and rebuild them from scratch, with modern plumbing and electricity. Funds came from family members who live in the West, and savings from sweater selling and other jobs. It was obvious that through hard work the Tibetans had become successful.

I asked one of the neighbors what would happen with their house when they moved back to Tibet. She told me, impromptu, that the Indian people have been so kind to the Tibetans that she would be very happy to give her house to an Indian family. I was amazed to hear her say that. It seemed to me nearly inconceivable to hear a non-Tibetan echo such gratitude and kindness. This evidence of spontaneous compassion is no doubt due to the Dalai Lama's influence. The Dalai Lama's modesty, openness, giving nature, and emphasis on nonattachment is clearly reflected in the Tibetan people.

Through superb embroidery, textiles are transformed into visionary experience.

A Tibetan woman is embroidering a ceremonial robe for a monk dance ritual.

SELF-SUPPORTING PEOPLE

Not all Tibetans in exile live in settlements in India. Many live in scattered communities in India and Nepal where they maintain their culture through frequent contact with each other. For my part, I couldn't always tell the difference between those living in settlements and those who didn't. The more Tibetans I met and interacted with, the more common traits I began to see. The Tibetan spirit is strong wherever the Tibetans live. The Dalai Lama's effort at creating cohesion is visible.

It is hard to imagine Kalimpong was once a major trading outpost for the Tibetans along the Silk Route. The two parallel roads, one for people and a second for load-carrying animals, still run through what was the center of town. Before 1959, wood was exported from Tibet to India along with white yak tails, used by Indians for their *puja*, or ceremonial worship. The Tibetans operated inns and cafes and lived along a stretch of town center, dubbed the "tenth mile" route. After 1959, when trade between India and Tibet was shut down, Kalimpong fell into decline and is now a desolate place. The few remaining Tibetans work in cottage industries molding incense, sewing cotton and brocade boots used in monk dances, and adding fringe to kata scarves. Although these are self-supporting people, there is a settlement officer who looks after a number of these communities, including Kalimpong. Jampal Kalden, who is a member of the local assembly, has lived here since 1956. He looks after those who are destitute, the elderly, and those who are unable to care for themselves. Tibetan doctors make monthly house calls. Tibetans who live outside of settlements have fewer networks and social services provided for them than those who live in settlements. However, when they need support, they can count on the CTA: they are not forgotten or alone. Samdong Rinpoche explained the difference between living in a settlement versus being self-supporting.

> *Kalimpong is not a settlement. Some of the people who are living there arrived before 1959. They are traders—businessmen. After some years, these people founded a cooperative society. They opened a school. They've lived like this for a long time and are not willing to move to a settlement. But they are not able to get all of the facilities from CTA—only a bit of help.*

I went from Kalimpong to Darjeeling, another town where many Tibetans have lived and continue to live. The contrast between Darjeeling, a neighboring city built in the Himalayan foothills, and Kalimpong could not be greater. Darjeeling was once a summer resort for the British Raj elite and is now a popular vacation site for middle-class Indians. It is still known for the black tea grown in the mountains and for the Darjeeling Himalayan Railway. I had wanted to travel on this historic train, but was warned that with all the scheduled stops, the ten-mile trip would take a whole day. As it was, the car ride along the railroad tracks took an hour. Seeing Darjeeling for the first time was a disappointment. I had an image of a lush green village on a hill. In sharp contrast to my romantic image, Darjeeling was overcrowded, noisy, and polluted. The colonial town was originally designed for 10,000 inhabitants, but with its current population of more than ten times that, the infrastructure is about to burst. Many of the Tibetans here live in apartments in large concrete buildings. Where there are many Tibetans, the ubiquitous prayer flags can be seen on roofs. In contrast to those living in Kalimpong, the Tibetans in Darjeeling are successful. A Tibetan-run shopping center near the town center provides a good variety of boutiques catering to Indian tourists. Their success? They import clothing from Bangkok, so the fashion is unique. Most of the stores are run by young Tibetans. I suspect that many young people from Kalimpong move here after graduating from school.

The Tibetans have a network of social services in Darjeeling as well. The settlement officer takes care of the elders who do not have families and those who are destitute. He said the Tibetan entrepreneurs have assimilated into the Indian culture and speak Nepalese, English, or Hindi, even with each other. He was afraid they had forgotten their Tibetan heritage until, he noted, the protest in Tibet during the Olympics in 2008 triggered their cultural identity. Many of them went to the border towns to participate in peaceful rallies against the treatment of Tibetans. Some tried to enter Tibet but were turned back at the border. He realized that being Tibetan is more than sharing a common language; it's something in the mind and heart and cannot be taken away.

The settlement officer explained why and how he ended up working for the exiled government. He said people from his region of Kham believe the Dalai Lama is the Buddha, and not a human being. One day when he was twelve years old, his uncle made him promise not to tell anyone about a gathering he was invited to. After promising, he was taken to a hidden place where a few Tibetans were watching a video. When he saw the Dalai Lama walking and talking to his people, it had a powerful effect on him; he felt he had to see the Dalai Lama in person.

Shortly afterwards, he escaped to India with a group of monks. Two weeks after arriving in Dharamsala, they were granted an audience with the Dalai Lama. As is customary, each of them was given new names to signify rebirth. Tenzin Nobling told the Dalai Lama, now that he had met him, that he would go back to Tibet. When the Dalai Lama offered to send him to school instead, he decided to stay in India, a decision he is happy to have made. After graduating from an Indian University, he was hired by the Tibetan government. When the Dalai Lama visited Hunsur, he was the settlement officer there. The Dalai Lama remembered him and told him he was particularly happy to see young Tibetans work for the exiled government.

On my way to the Tibetan Refugee Self Help Center, located outside the city, I caught a glimpse of the Darjeeling that was imprinted in my mind. The fog hovered over the top of the mountain range, revealing the lush green valley below. The Center was founded in 1959 by Gyalo Thondup, the Dalai Lama's older brother, as an emergency relief center for refugees. Over a hundred Tibetans are engaged in making Tibetan handicrafts. The craftspeople spin, dye, and weave wool for carpets, carve wood to make furniture and book covers, and paint Buddhist art. I ordered a small rug with the eight auspicious Buddhist symbols. The wool for the carpet was dyed in colors made from tea leaves, turmeric, and other organic plants. It takes a month to weave one small carpet. A retired carpet weaver invited me to visit her one room apartment, painted in a striking bright turquoise. It is part of a complex that houses ten retirees. Nearby, there is a large apartment building housing 105 families. In addition to housing, the Center maintains a day care as well as a healthcare facility for the employees.

Lingtsang is another self-supporting community located in a small village in Dehradun, Uttarakhand. The Tibetans who live there are engaged in a small cottage industry forging bronze ceremonial objects. They work in collaboration, with different households specializing in one or more aspects of the process. The less skilled perform simpler tasks while the most skilled tune the metal so that the sounds produce a clear resonance. In every household, two of the most seen objects in Tibetan art and monasteries—pieces of *vajra* (thunderbolt), symbol of skillful means and the *tribu* (bell), symbol of wisdom—are in various stages of completion. I wanted to purchase a *vajra* and *tribu*, but they told me every item was accounted for. Years later when I bought them from a monk in Oakland, I fondly remembered the community where these were forged. Their prosperity demonstrates that the Tibetan diaspora has successfully developed their own international trade.

As the diaspora adapted to modernization and took on new roles and occupations, the Dalai Lama became the glue that held this diverse mosaic together under the big Tibetan tent. This enabled the Tibetans to adapt to their new lives while strengthening their identity as Tibetans. One of the successes the Dalai Lama is most happy with is that the people of the diaspora now identify first as Tibetans instead of by their region or by their trade. In exile, not only has the Dalai Lama prevented the loss of Tibetan culture, but he has strengthened it by reinforcing the core tenets of being Tibetan while modernizing what needed to change.

Man carving an incised wood manuscript cover. Manuscript covers evoke the dimensionality of the text they contain.

Spun wool is woven into designs of remarkable intricacy and beauty. These artworks bear designs associated with different aspects of Tibetan societies. By creating carpets, the Tibetan community preserves and projects its culture.

Tibetans from the west travel to attend the Dalai Lama's teachings.

TIBETANS IN THE WEST

Switzerland was the first European country to offer asylum to Tibetan refugees. Because there were so many orphans, the Dalai Lama asked his Swiss friend to find families who would care for them. Between 1961 and 1981 the Swiss government invited 1,000 refugees to settle there. The first group of refugees who went there were orphans who were raised as Swiss in Swiss families. Traveling to Switzerland from Tibet must have felt like going to a different planet. Lacking German and technical skills, most Tibetan refugees worked in factories. Switzerland still has the largest number of Tibetans in Europe; many of whom are third generation— grandchildren to the first immigrants. Have they preserved their culture? Samdhong Rinpoche, the first Prime Minister of the Tibetan government-in-exile, said:

> *I used to say, sarcastically to Tibetans living in the West, that other people are worried about preservation of our culture and language. So don't worry, Western people will preserve our culture. They are more interested than you. And one day the Tibetan people will have to go to an American or an Indian professor to learn about Tibetan Buddhism. I used to challenge them this way.*

But he sees hope. Samdhong Rinpoche believes somewhere deep inside each Tibetan the seeds of their culture have been planted and will remain. He said:

> *Tibetan children who are born and brought up in the West are losing their language very fast. But after some time, they are coming back. This is my personal experience. Many Tibetans settled in Switzerland in the early 1970s. I visited Switzerland in 1977. The whole younger generation below the age of 20 had become completely Swiss. They didn't know how to greet a monk or a senior person. They said, "hi" and shook hands. So, I thought the younger generation was finished. That was my impression.*

> *Then I visited again in 1991. Those who had become Swiss in the 1970s were in their thirties and forties. At that age they were trying to learn the Tibetan language and were attending Buddhist courses.*

They no longer just said "hi" but folded their hands to greet me.

I thought there must be some seed in their mind that re-emerges after a certain age. It may not be 100%, but most of their language comes back. Maybe it's too late to be totally proficient but still they are trying to remain Tibetans. This kind of feeling is coming back.

The Office of Tibet was established in New York in 1964 to keep alive the issue of Tibet in the United Nations. At that time, there were only a handful of Tibetans living in the United States who had emigrated there on their own. In addition to the government officials, there were a few Tibetan Buddhist teachers, as well as lumberjacks in Maine—an experiment that failed as the Tibetans are small in stature and didn't have the ability to do this work—and students attending universities. The 1990 Immigration Act granted 1,000 visas to displaced Tibetans living in India and in Nepal. Fearing the loss of Tibetan culture should they be dispersed throughout the USA, Tibetans were resettled in close proximity in twenty-one cluster sites in eighteen different states. The largest communities are in New York, New Jersey, Minnesota, California, Oregon, Washington, and Colorado. In contrast to the Tibetans in the settlements in India and in Nepal, those who emigrated to the West are the younger generation seeking job opportunities. Almost every city with even a small Tibetan population has a community center where Tibetans meet to celebrate Tibetan New Year, the Dalai Lama's birthday, and attend teachings from visiting Tibetan monks. On Sundays, these centers offer courses in Tibetan language, culture, religion, dance, and music for Tibetan children. They also serve as a place for elders to practice Buddhism as a community.

About 100 Tibetans live in Santa Fe. I went to see the newly built community center one Sunday and found children studying Tibetan culture and language. A high school student who immigrated from India to the USA about two years ago was helping younger children with the Tibetan alphabet while an instructor was teaching the older children. I asked her how her life differs from those of her American classmates. She said that her parents are much stricter than her friends' parents—they expect her to get all A's whereas her friends' parents are happy if they pass. She studies during and week and on weekends she teaches Tibetan writing at the Tibetan community center. She said she wants to serve the community and is aspiring to be a doctor. With her motivation, focus, and study habits, no doubt she will achieve her goal.

In Queens, New York, where there is a large Tibetan population, Tibetan elders study Buddhism with an impassioned young monk who had been sent there from his monastery in southern India. He posed questions, but whenever they didn't have the answer, they said, "We are old; our memory is not good." He gently scolded them, saying "Age is not an excuse for not studying." This comment is always followed by laughter. The founder of the senior center said that when he moved to New York from India with his mother, she was afraid to go out of the house. She had no one to talk to during the day while he was away at work. He found her getting more and more depressed. When he discovered other Tibetans had the same problem with their elderly parents, they pooled their resources and rented a community hall so their parents could socialize. As more people joined, they were able to invite a Tibetan monk to give Buddhist teachings. When he found that many of the elders suffered from hypertension, they started to provide a vegetarian lunch five days a week. Now, his mother looks forward to Mondays when she can join her friends at the community center.

These centers are critical to preserving Tibetan culture. Sonam Gyatso, past president of The Tibetan Community of New York & New Jersey (TCNYNJ), explained:

> Our children spend more time with their American friends and less time with their parents, so in twenty or so years their children probably won't be able to speak any Tibetan. This is a critical situation in the Tibetan society. If we don't have an organization like this, there is a threat to our identity. Once we lose our culture, we will lose our identity and then there is no use fighting for the freedom of Tibet.

With such weighty responsibility, the Tibetan diaspora works hard to keep the Tibetan culture and spirit alive. Whenever the Dalai Lama holds international public teachings, he has private meetings with the Tibetans. Sonam Gyatso explained why he thought it possible for Tibetans to preserve their culture while most other immigrant groups have become acculturated.

> Compared with other nations, we have the Buddhist religion in common. We are bonded very tight. The root of Tibetan culture is ancient Tibetan Buddhism. As long as Tibetan Buddhism remains in the world, there will be Tibetan culture. There is a parallel with Judaism. As Jews they stay together.

Tibetan monks constructing sand mandala to transmit positive energy over the course of many days. It is then dismantled, symbolising the Buddhist belief in the transitory nature of life.

We Tibetans try to stay together. We stay physically close. Wherever there are fifteen or more Tibetans, there is a Tibetan association. People from other cultures are on their own and as the years go by, they are assimilated.

As Tibetan refugees moved from India and Nepal to the West, they have had to adapt to their host cultures, since the economic system is not developed for them the way it is in the Tibetan settlements in India and in Nepal. Tibetan immigrants who had worked as teachers, government workers, and settlement officers in India, now work in grocery stores or as nannies or caregivers in senior homes. Despite their modest, low-skill jobs, they say America has given them a home; they are no longer displaced. They feel they have the freedom to keep the Tibet issue alive in the global consciousness. In India, Tibetans are issued Residency Certificates (RC) and do not have passports, as Tibetans are stateless. Perhaps more importantly, Tibetans who live in the West say there is more opportunity for their children. The skills they acquired in the settlements have enabled them to build community centers, develop social projects for the elders, and set up weekend cultural and educational programs for their children.

Many younger Tibetans born in the West cannot speak their native language fluently. The differences between the graying population and the youth widen as the latter become steadily immersed in the popular culture, media, values, languages, thought and education systems of the nations where they live. I asked a Tibetan woman, who immigrated from India to California, if she is afraid her children will become acculturated and forget they are Tibetans. She told me there is no fear her son will lose his culture. She said, when they first immigrated to the USA and he started schooling, he was constantly being bullied. During recess, the boys would deliberately stomp on ants, reducing him to tears. Throughout this nearly daily ordeal, the Tibetan boy vowed he would not fight back but would practice patience. I asked him how he withstood the bullying for so long. He said he kept in mind the Dalai Lama's teaching of the Middle Way and kept up a dialogue with the "bully." His patience was rewarded. In second grade, the "bully" became his best friend, telling others not to stomp on insects. By living their lives and practicing the same values as if they were in Tibet, Tibetans in the West are preserving the vision of the Dalai Lama and their Tibetan culture.

MODERNIZING TIBETAN CULTURE

The modernization of the Tibetan culture was envisioned by the Dalai Lama and built organically by the organizations he created with help from the people who followed him into exile. The Dalai Lama's vision has transformed every aspect of Tibetan society—from central and local governments and education and monastic practices to the study and practice of Tibetan Buddhism by lay people. Tibetan traditions are now suited to the modern world, thus keeping Tibetan culture alive. After more than sixty years, the Tibet issue is still alive and clearly in the hands of the Tibetan people and their organizations, which means the struggle will continue whether His Holiness is alive or not, and whether the Dalai Lama Institute remains. This is the explicit design of the Dalai Lama.

The Dalai Lama has strengthened the unity of the Tibetan diaspora so that their identities are less with their own regions—Amdo, Central, and Kham—and more as Tibetans. Wherever he built organizations, he trained leaders. Central to Tibetan Buddhism is the training of one's mind to turn adversity into advantage and transform problems into opportunities to gain inner strength, as well as to develop patience and to practice tolerance. This process has enabled Tibetans to maintain their dignity and spirit in the face of difficulties. The Tibetan community has risen to the challenge, transforming adverse circumstances with great determination and enthusiasm. Their ordinary family and monastic life have continued in the wake of cultural catastrophes.

The Dalai Lama educated the children, so they have the knowledge and the skills to live in the modern world. He made sure the children know what Tibetan culture is—for they are the custodians for the preservation of this culture. The education developed under the guidance of the Dalai Lama focuses on building inner strength— truth, honesty, justness, transparency—and spirituality—warm heartedness and compassion.

The transfer of political destiny of Tibetans away from the Dalai Lama to a democratic government will ensure the Dalai Lama's intellectual, scientific, philosophical, and spiritual legacy will transcend many generations into the future. Through the leadership of the Dalai Lama, the Tibetan diaspora has had the necessary security and mental peace to preserve their culture and religion and educate new generations to face the challenges of tomorrow. Tibetans, under the vision of the Dalai Lama, are breathing new life into their traditions and projecting them far beyond any geographic boundaries. In the twenty-first century, Tibetan Buddhism has traveled to all parts of the world.

Tibetans have told me that refugees from other countries have said they envy them because they have the Dalai Lama as their leader. Tibetans tell me they now share the Dalai Lama with the rest of the world. They are right! And, how lucky we are!

Student painting traditional thangka, an ancient Tibetan art form which depicts Buddhist deities.

Tibetan Institute of Performing Arts was established to preserve Tibetan opera, dance and music.

To the right of the Dalai Lama's throne is a statue of Padmasambava Guru Rinpoche, who brought Buddhism to Tibet in the eighth century.

THE DALAI LAMA'S STORY: SPIRITUAL LEADER

The Dalai Lama is the beloved leader of the Tibetan people and their Buddhist faith. The Tibetan people are deeply devoted to him. I witnessed their dedication the first time I attended the Dalai Lama's Buddhist teaching and empowerment lesson in 2006. The *Kalachakra*, or Wheel of Life, empowerment is extremely important as practitioners of the Kalachakra must be initiated by a qualified teacher before practicing it. Tibetans aspire to attend at least one Kalachakra empowerment in their lifetime. This one had added significance as it was held by the Dalai Lama in the same location where the Buddha gave his first Kalachakra sermon in the fifth century BCE. Amravati is therefore considered to be one of the most sacred Buddhist pilgrimage centers in India.

The Dalai Lama received his Kalachakra empowerment from his senior tutor, Ling Rinpoche, in 1953 during a period of fragile rapprochement with the Chinese authorities. He wrote in his autobiography that he felt "extremely privileged to be participating in a tradition performed over countless generations by successions of highly realized spiritual masters."[3] While chanting the last verse, he was so moved he was choked with emotions. The following year, the Dalai Lama received full ordination in front of the statue of Avalokiteshvara and that summer he gave his first Kalachakra empowerment ceremony followed with a second one in 1957; this was two years before going into exile in 1959.

The Dalai Lama knows how important it is for him to visit and give teachings to the Tibetan diaspora. He has given a total of thirty-two Kalachakra initiations in exile, more than any of his predecessors. He has given twenty-one Kalachakra initiations in India, either in one of the Settlements, Dharamsala, or at sacred Buddhist sites. Ten Kalachakra empowerment events were held in Western countries where large numbers of Tibetans have made their homes—Rikon in Switzerland, Madison, Los Angeles, New York, Bloomington, Washington D.C., and Toronto, as well as in cities in Australia, Austria, and Spain.

Not only was this the first time I had ever attended the Dalai Lama's Buddhist teachings, at the time, I had yet to meet any Tibetans. The first time I met

Tibetans was on the twelve-hour train ride from Hyderabad to Amravati. I was feeling slightly uncomfortable traveling alone in a train full of Indian men. Fortunately, a Tibetan family, who was also going to the teachings, invited me to join them in their compartment. One of the Tibetan young men stood up and gave me his seat. I would learn that this gesture of kindness is their usual mode of operation. Once we arrived, we headed our separate ways. The Tibetan family went looking for their relatives while I went to the conference center to see about getting a press pass which would allow me to photograph. After obtaining a press pass, I took a tuk-tuk to find the campsite to which I was assigned. Driving by acres of fields filled with thousands of tents, I began to realize how important this empowerment is to the Tibetans.

Every morning, I walked for half an hour on a dusty road from my campsite to the temple where the teaching took place. My tent was a simple one with two single beds. The facilities were located at the edge of the campsite. A much larger canvas tent where food was served was in the middle of the campsite. Luxury tents with bedrooms and bathrooms were at the campsites closer to the temple. I was amazed to see such a diverse group of people walking towards the temple. As we got closer to the temple, we could hear the Dalai Lama's distinct baritone chant. The majority of the 100,000 pilgrims consisted of Tibetans from Tibet and the Tibetan diaspora from India, Nepal, and the West, and Buddhists from the Himalaya regions and other parts of Asia, including an unprecedented 400 Chinese from China. There were also Buddhist practitioners from the West. As the empowerment was requested by the Bushokai, a Japanese Buddhist group, there were quite a few Japanese devotees of the Dalai Lama. Altogether, people from seventy-one nations attended. The Dalai Lama spoke in Tibetan and was simultaneously translated into multiple languages including English, Japanese, Korean, Italian, Russian, Mandarin, Telugu, the local Indian language, as well as the Tibetan Amdo and Kham dialects, which is where most of the Tibetans come from.

As more and more Tibetans arrived, they set up food stalls and cafes along the road from the campsites to the temple site. Stalls selling incense, prayer wheels and beads, jewelry, and other items were set up by Tibetans from Tibet. In no time, this sleepy town came to life!

On the first day, I was stunned to find a three-tiered stage housed under a magnificent, elaborately decorated tent. A makeshift temple was built on the stage to accommodate the sand mandala, which was created for this occasion, and the Dalai Lama's teaching and practice thrones. As a member of the press, I entered through a side entrance, where I had my photography gear inspected. We sat to the side of the stage from where we could only see the Dalai Lama's profile, but we were allowed to wander around the path between barriers to photograph and to videotape. Despite the crowd, it was well organized. Areas were clustered off, so everyone knew where they were meant to sit. The Tibetans, of course, had been to the Dalai Lama's teachings, so they knew to bring cushions to sit on. Special guests sat on the stage. The senior monks and nuns sat directly facing the Dalai Lama, and the novices sat behind the monks and nuns, so there was a huge sea of red. Tibetan pilgrims sat behind and beside the monastic population. International visitors were to the right of the stage separated by the language that they spoke, which was beamed by radio for that section. Not only did this arrangement make those listening to the radio hear better, after the daily teaching, the Dalai Lama greeted us by our nationality. His energy level was astonishing.

The Kalachakra is one of the most important initiations in the Tibetan Buddhist tradition and has special significance for world peace. This teaching is based on a classic text, so the Dalai Lama's discourse was a world away from his more informal public talks where he generally speaks about the promotion of human value, universal responsibility in the modern world, and the promotion of religious harmony. In fact, the discourse was difficult. However, as I started to attend more of his teachings, I began to see his style. He is an incredibly learned scholar, and his Buddhist teachings reflect his brilliant mind. He is skillful in making his teachings come alive by highlighting key points by using a more informal style. One afternoon, we were all given kusha grass, often used in Buddhist rituals due to its symbolic significance, to put under our pillows. The next day, the Dalai Lama asked us if we had any dreams. Those of us who had vivid dreams felt special—like having the Jedi force within us, and those who didn't felt slightly left out. Then the Dalai Lama said, if we had dreams, not to hold on to them and if we didn't, that's fine. With those simple words, he cut away the illusions of self-grandeur we held onto.

The Dalai Lama opened the Kalachakra ceremony by telling the 15,000 Tibetans, who had been given permission to attend by the Chinese government, that he considered them as the main audience for the Kalachakra because he knew they have suffered tremendously and are less fortunate than the Tibetan diaspora. They must have felt tremendously happy. Not only did the Dalai Lama single them out, but many of them were able to see their families for the first time in years. The Dalai Lama urged them to let others know the importance of the

"Middle Way" approach towards the Tibet issue. He called on the Tibetans who were not able to attend to join in prayers and visualize and generate compassion on the three days of the empowerment, adding, "Receiving of blessings does not depend on the distance but on one's devotion and dedication."

It was scorching hot, yet the Tibetans were dressed in layers of their finest, often adorned with the fur of wild animals. The Dalai Lama thanked them for wearing their finest but pleaded with them to change into something more comfortable or to take off a few layers to avert heatstroke. He then told them that it was regrettable to see them adorn their clothing with fur and added that they must protect and not kill wildlife. I vividly recall the wide-eyed, bewildered looks on their faces. In the nearly fifty years in exile, the Dalai Lama had transformed into a twenty-first century monk. I couldn't tell if the Tibetans were thunderstruck from seeing and hearing the Dalai Lama in person, as some still believed him to be a Buddha, or if they were simply captivated by the modern and friendly Dalai Lama who had told them about the importance of science and to understand Buddhism through logic and not to rely on superstition. Regardless, they consider him their leader, so when they got back to Tibet, they burned their fur trimmings and have stopped wearing fur.

I witnessed the Tibetan people's deep devotion to the Dalai Lama. They believe he is the manifestation of Avalokiteshvara, the *bodhisattva* of universal compassion. *Bodhi* means wisdom that understands the ultimate nature of reality, and *sattva* is a person motivated by universal compassion. Thus, a bodhisattva is a being who is engaged on the path toward Buddhahood and is devoted to helping all sentient beings to become liberated from suffering. The Dalai Lama has said that he lives his life by following the bodhisattva ideal, and his aspiration is to practice infinite compassion with infinite wisdom. This daily practice of compassion and wisdom surely reinforces their belief.

I also witnessed the Dalai Lama lead by the power of *nying je chenmo*, which means great compassion in Tibetan. He has enhanced his sensitivity towards others' suffering by opening himself to it, as he witnessed the devastation his people suffered in Tibet. He has dedicated himself entirely to helping others overcome their suffering and the causes of their suffering. This advanced state of spiritual development pushes compassion to the highest level and acts as a powerful inspiration. Doing so has given meaning and purpose to his life and has had a domino effect where others, both Tibetans and non-Tibetans, have taken up similar goals and multiplied the effort.

As a spiritual leader, first of the Tibetans, then for humanity, the Dalai Lama's definition of spirituality is broad and inclusive. He reinforced this in 2017, at the thirty-fourth Kalachakra Empowerment. He told the over 200,000 attendees, "You have all come here with great enthusiasm to listen to the dharma. Let's turn it into an opportunity to do practice. Whatever religious tradition you follow, what's important is to be sincere about it. The main practice of all our various traditions is the cultivation of altruism—a sense of love and compassion." He then added, "What we need to do is to change our outlook and focus on the welfare of others. Since you've gone to the effort and expense of coming here, while you're here try to make some inner transformation." He warned us that we can't do this through prayer alone; we must use our mind and transform it. And it will take time.

These principles stem from a strong ethical sense and following them is a way to increase happiness and peace. Even His Holiness' spirituality is pragmatic. He is a spiritual leader, both by being an adept Buddhist practitioner and teacher and by being a role model.

The Dalai Lama ordaining monks in his private temple.

PRESERVING TIBETAN BUDDHIST CULTURE

Years ago, at a press conference in Basel, Switzerland, a young Tibetan journalist asked the Dalai Lama, "Do you expect us to go back to Tibet when it becomes free?" The Dalai Lama's reply was, "No, you don't need to be in Tibet to be a Tibetan. You can preserve the Tibetan culture wherever you are. And by culture, I do not mean just the language or the dance. It must be deeper." As my journey to photograph the Tibetan diaspora took me around the world, it was this deeper culture that I wanted to understand. I had the opportunity to ask the Dalai Lama in person. This was his reply:

> Tibetan Culture is not a few dances—like the sacred mask dance. These are minor. Real Tibetan culture is deeper knowledge. One night, I dreamt I met people and was explaining quantum physics— that the Buddhist concept of emptiness is relevant. The best language is Tibetan so the world should learn Tibetan!

> These concepts originally came from India, but only Tibetans have kept this knowledge. That is what we consider to be Tibetan culture. Now in India, there is not much knowledge about these things. Cultural heritage is not just religious faith but knowledge. And then there is logic. Ancient Indian logic is very rich.

Tibetan culture is inextricably interwoven with Tibetan Buddhist philosophy, which represents the authentic Nalanda tradition with its rigorous study of philosophy and psychology based on reason and logic. Among the different Buddhist traditions, only Tibetans employ the Indian discipline of reasoning and logic in their studies. The Dalai Lama continued:

> The Nalanda tradition seems to be the most comprehensive presentation of the Buddha's teachings available today. It incorporates knowledge of the mind and emotions, which is of potential benefit to all humanity. From this tradition I have learnt the correct view of reality and how to train my mind by tackling my disturbing emotions.

Monks and novices are enjoying the gathering and the dance.

The Tibetan long horn and the oboe are played at certain times in the rite, especially when deities manifest in our ordinary world.

Monks adopt the body of a deity and dance that divinity into manifestation. Masks are transformative devices that change people into the characters they represent. These dances take place in a setting where people gather. Tibetans use art in motion to activate the mythic

How did Tibetan culture become so tied in with the Indian Nalanda tradition of Buddhism? Buddhism flourished in the eighth century during the reign of King Trisong Detsen (756–ca.800 CE), who invited the great scholar and abbot of India's Nalanda Monastery, Shantarakshita, to teach in Tibet. It is for this reason the root of Tibetan Buddhism is based on the Indian monastic Nalanda University. Since Tibet by then had its own written language, which was based on the Indian alphabet with the addition of vowels and consonants, Shantarakshita advised the Tibetans to translate Buddhist literature from Indian into Tibetan. These writings have been preserved in the Tibetan tradition as *Kangyur*, the translation of the words of the Buddha, and the *Tengyur*, translation of Indian master's commentaries. The Nalanda tradition of Buddhism was spreading throughout Tibet as it was declining in India. Under Shantarakshita's direction, monasteries were built and Tibetan monks were ordained. Tibet then became the custodian of India's ancient Buddhism and has kept it alive through extensive and rigorous study, debates, continuing commentaries, and its application in daily life.

Tibetan Buddhism incorporates knowledge of the mind and emotions; it represents a path of transforming the mind with the aim of freeing ourselves from suffering and the causes of suffering. It is a collection of teachings for building inner peace through an expansion of consciousness and the infinite potential of the mind. Buddha taught the path to liberation and awakening but expected people to deepen their faith through study, investigation, and analysis—not just to memorize scriptural quotations. The Dalai Lama says he habitually contemplates—reflecting and analyzing what he has read. However, he doesn't stop there because at this point it is an intellectual exercise. He internalizes the teachings by observing his emotions, and in this way, the teachings come alive and are applied to his life. He explains that peace of mind can be developed through mind training. He has said, living within the principles of the dharma provides direction and purpose. Its main objective is to cultivate genuine concern for the well-being of others and become kind-hearted people. Buddhism also emphasizes individual responsibility.

The Dalai Lama is one of the world's foremost Tibetan Buddhist scholars, trained in the Nalanda tradition of Indian Buddhism. He is also an exceptional spiritual teacher. He takes his role as the spiritual leader of Tibetans extremely seriously and has strengthened the practice of Buddhism among the Tibetan diasporas. His teaching schedule is intense. As a Buddhist teacher, he attracts many Tibetan Buddhist monks and nuns as well as lay people. Samdhong Rinpoche explained:

The Dalai Lama said Buddha Dharma and Buddhist philosophy is not only for monks—it's for everyone. It's for lay people, women—everyone can study it. The survival of Tibetan Buddhism doesn't entirely depend on monks and nuns. It depends on every Tibetan.

He often teaches Tibetan youth. In one of his introductory talks on Buddhism given to the students at the Tibetan Children's Village, the Dalai Lama told them that although the Nalanda tradition has spread throughout Tibet, most Tibetans did not appreciate it fully, repeating scripture quotations without comprehending the tradition that relies on investigation and analysis. He told the students that they should not accept his teachings out of faith but must use reasoning and logic to determine what they believe in.

A Tibetan who has immigrated to the United States told me that non-Tibetans like to study Buddhism whereas Tibetans don't study but practice by reciting the

Student monks engaging in philosophical debate to enhance their learning.

mantra. And while this may have been true for many Tibetans, the Dalai Lama is working to change these habits. Samdhong Rinpoche explained that the Dalai Lama is encouraging Tibetans to study.

> *His Holiness always says, without study, how are you practicing? Without knowing the theory, how are you practicing? For any serious practitioners having only faith is not enough. Study! The younger Tibetan generation are also studying more. And older people are also debating. This was unknown in Tibet. His Holiness says people should not just believe, but study, debate, and have a rational mind. In Hunsur settlement twenty elder women demonstrated their debating skills in front of the Dalai Lama. This is all new.*

The Dalai Lama wants Tibetans to understand and appreciate the Nalanda Buddhist tradition by studying and thinking about the teachings, discussing, and debating the ideas presented, not just blindly reciting mantras. He believes that a deeper understanding and practice of Tibetan Buddhism will have a positive effect on the practitioner. In one of his numerous teachings at the main temple in Dharamsala, he explained how to achieve happiness:

> *Whenever sentient beings think of themselves, they have a sense of "I" in relation to their body and mind, their family, and friends. Human beings have a sense of "I" as the controller of their psycho-physical aggregates. But Buddhist teaching rejects any such objective existence of the self. It rejects any perception of a solidified existent "I."*

> *If you only think of yourself, you put yourself at a disadvantage. If, instead, you open your heart and extend your concern to others, you'll be free of fear and anxiety. If you think of all sentient beings as being like you in not wanting suffering, self-cherishing will be reduced. Look at those around you. Those who are respectful and concerned about others tend to be happier, those who are more self-centered are less so. Think of those who share their sweets and whatever good things they have and those who keep them to themselves—which of them seems to be happier?*

As a spiritual heir to the Nalanda system of logic and reasoning, the Dalai Lama has enhanced the quality of spirituality among the Tibetan people.

Although Tibetan culture has been highly influenced by Tibetan Buddhism, it is more than Buddhism. The Tibetan way of life is one of compassion, non-violence, and peace and is applied to all sentient beings, that is any living thing that has a mind, and to the environment. Tibetans have developed a distinct culture due to the geographic isolation and harsh climate of their home country. Remoteness and high altitude living precipitated a unique and a simpler way of life. And though natural resources are limited, there is more than enough for everyone in the sparsely populated country. No one takes more than is needed. The Dalai Lama explains the respect Tibetans have toward their environment, which includes planet earth. It is based on the view of interdependence.

Our unique environment has strongly influenced us. We don't live on a small, heavily populated island. Historically, we have had little anxiety with our vast area, low population, and distant neighbors.

The Tibetan Buddhist attitude is one of contentment, and there may be some connection here with our attitude toward the environment. We don't indiscriminately consume—we put a limit on our consumption. We admire simple living and individual responsibility. We have always considered ourselves as part of our environment, but not just any part. Our ancient scriptures speak of the container and the contained. The world is the container—our house and we are the contained—the contents of the container.

From these simple facts we deduce a special relationship, because without the container, the contents cannot be contained. Without the contents, the container contains nothing; it's meaningless. [4]

The belief in reincarnation also reinforces the Tibetan culture of caring for the environment. If we believe that we will be reborn, we are more likely to preserve nature.

Novice monk practicing ume, a unique alphabet used in the monasteries.

The Nechung Oracle, the state oracle of Tibet, in a trance to see into the future. The regalia enhances and embodies the altered state of awareness into which the medium enters. On his chest is an oracle mirror. The silver is a symbol of a pristine mind devoid of content which allows for entry into the oracular state of consciousness.

PRESERVING ANCIENT TRADITIONS

Culture is people, art, religion, performance—it's woven from many elements. Cultural narratives are enacted in full through gatherings and ceremonies, with full participation of the community. One of the most important ceremonies during the Losar (Tibetan New Year) celebration is the Dalai Lama's private new year audience with the protector oracles. The Tibetan oracles are steeped in cultural traditions. The Dalai Lama recalled his introduction to his "spirit" protector when he was five years old. As the Dalai Lama, he said he is compelled to preserve this tradition. He explained:

> Since my childhood, since I was a five-year-old, the Nechung Oracle has been close to me. I appreciate these beings, provided they are authentic. Sometimes they are not authentic and are evil spirits. It is very important to make the distinctions and examine them carefully. These mysterious spirits have developed special connections with King Trison Detsen since the eighth century. The previous thirteen Dalai Lamas have all had some special connections; so, as a person who has the name of Dalai Lama, I must keep these traditions alive.

One of the protector divinities of the Dalai Lama is manifested through the Nechung Oracle who has protected the Dalai Lama throughout the years. After having told the Dalai Lama to stay in Tibet for many years, the Nechung Oracle suddenly told the Dalai Lama to escape. The Dalai Lama said:

> In 1957 or 1958 the Oracle said to me, a time will come when you feel despondent. There is a broad river which we usually cross by horseback. I will extend a bridge for you to cross the river. Finally, on March 16, 1959, he said, "Now is the time. Go, you should leave Lhasa. The usual sort of road is very safe. You can go that way. So, quite nice."

Two days after the Dalai Lama's escape, his palace was bombed. Had he not escaped, he would have been killed by the Chinese military.

Seeing the Dalai Lama sitting on his throne, which is essentially a large platform with an equally large cushion, wearing the ceremonial yellow hat of the Gelug school of Tibetan Buddhism, with which he is associated, gave me a slight glimpse of how he might have appeared in Lhasa. Cabinet members sat on cushions placed on patterned Tibetan carpets to his left. Monks from the Dalai Lama's personal monastery, Namgyal Monastery, sat at the back and side of the room, chanting prayers to the sound of drums, horns, and cymbals. The intense smell and smoke of incense filled the room. Suddenly, Thupten Ngodup, the Medium through whom the Nechung Oracle speaks, whom I met many years ago, entered with his attendants. I barely recognized the friendly monk. He looked spellbound. He was elaborately attired in layers of golden brocade with red, blue, green, white, and yellow patterns. He walked to the center of the temple room and sat on a stool facing the Dalai Lama. His attendants tightly belted an elaborate apron with colorful tassels, supporting flags and banners around his waist. They then placed a large, polished steel mirror surrounded by semi-precious stones around his neck. The monks chanted throughout, invoking the Nechung Oracle to enter the medium. It took over twenty minutes for the medium to fully enter a trance and for the Oracle to enter him. At that point, a towering ornate headdress was placed on his head. His face had turned red, and his eyes seemed focused on something distant. I wouldn't have recognized him had he come into the temple from that moment. Hissing, he leapt to his feet and postured with slow commanding steps, brandishing swords in both hands. Hardly able to contain his fierce energy, he moved towards the Dalai Lama, took a deep bow, and made ritual offerings before getting closer to him. His Holiness and the Nechung Oracle then bent their heads together—the former asked questions and the latter responded. Finally, the Oracle stomped back to his stool.

I was dazzled by the ornate costumes, the enchanting music, and the dances and rituals of the elaborate ceremony. I would have been stunned had I not been concentrating on capturing the fast-moving activities around me. At one point, one of the Dalai Lama's attendants spun me around so I could photograph activities on the other side of the temple. Cabinet members lined up, each posing questions to the Oracle. Before responding he jolted up, postured again, all the time hissing. At times the Nechung Oracle seemed to scold. At other times he seemed to instruct. One scribe furiously jotted his responses for later interpretation while another recorded the utterings. As soon as the Oracle had finished, he collapsed. The headdress, which weighed around thirty pounds, was quickly removed and he was carried out to the adjacent room to recover. His body was so rigid his attendants massaged his limbs to get his circulation flowing.

On this day, three State Oracles were consulted. The second Oracle consulted was Khandro-La, the State medium of the Tenma Oracle, the twelve guardian

The Nechung Oracle greeting the Dalai Lama.

deities of Tibetan Buddhism. Her attire was subdued in comparison with the Nechung Oracle. She had on layers of silver and gold brocade with embroidered patterns of red flowers on green stems. After quietly entering the temple room, she sat serenely, facing slightly to the right of the Dalai Lama. She took no time to enter a trance. A jeweled crown was placed on her head and a polished steel mirror, and several long strands of pearls were placed around her neck. Once the Tenma Oracle entered the medium, she became unrecognizable: her face puffed up, her eyes bulged and her tongue seemed to fill her whole mouth, giving her a wild look. She bowed to His Holiness, made a ritual offering, and then spoke with him. When she rose, the Dalai Lama held her hand, as if to steady her. The officials lined up to ask their questions. She too seemed to scold or instruct. She too collapsed into a rigid form and was carried out to the adjacent room to recover from the ordeal.

A third, the Gadhong Oracle, appeared to be the most wrathful of all, especially with his long black hair covering his face. He stomped about impatiently, acting and looking menacing. He also made ritual offerings to the Dalai Lama and kneeled in front of him. While all three Oracles were most humble toward the Dalai Lama, the Gadhong Oracle appeared only to scold the Cabinet members. After the mediums had rested, they were invited to join everyone present for tea. The medium for the Gadhong Oracle was still shaking from his trance. I was told most of the people don't understand the utterance of the Oracles. It is up to the scribe to translate the messages.

After the tea break, I was quickly escorted down the hill to a reception room where the Dalai Lama generally meets visitors. The first question he asked me was what I thought of the Oracles. Noticing I was speechless, he told me his response to Pico Iyer, his close friend and writer, when he asked how a person like him, with a scientific and logical mind, could consult oracles.

I told Pico Iyer there are different forms of life. I know this through my own experience. Indeed, I have a scientific mind, but I have some conviction of these things provided they are authentic. I told him; some sentient beings are different physically. We cannot see them. We can call them spirits or different kinds of beings. They have subtle bodies, and with subtle bodies they can go to different places. They can act as spies: they can go everywhere.

This was my introduction to the Dalai Lama.

The Dalai Lama with Khandro-La, the Tenma Oracle. Above him is a mural painting of Buddha Shakyamuni.

REESTABLISHING MONASTERIES

The study and practice of the Buddha's teachings were of primary importance in Tibet. Monasteries were lively places where monks were educated in Buddhist philosophy and art. Before the Chinese occupation of Tibet, it is estimated that twenty percent of the male population were monks and were among the most educated people in Tibet. The monastic institutions were so highly esteemed that at least one or two male children from every family entered the monastery. This means that eighty percent of the population supported all Tibetans. This structure was possible because of the lack of a military. The Great Fifth Dalai Lama created a unique monastic/secular-coordinated administration in 1642. The government demilitarized Tibet and officially formed it into a spiritual nation that supported Buddhist education.

The three great monasteries of Lhasa, founded in the fourteenth century, had a combined population of 20,000 monks. Their central role in establishing Tibetan culture cannot be overestimated. About twenty-five percent of the monks entered the twenty-year philosophy studies program which was built around five Indian texts and dealt with logic, ethics, cosmology, epistemology, and the path to enlightenment. The students memorized texts and commentaries and participated in debates where their understanding would be challenged. Monks who achieved high aptitude generally stayed on to teach. Scholarship was an equalizing factor: sons of farmers, nomads, and aristocrats—anyone could attain high levels of education and become teachers.

These monasteries also served as centers of Buddhism for the Himalayan world. Monks from Ladakh, Nepal, Mongolia, the Soviet Union, and all regions in Tibet enrolled in these monastic universities to receive education in Buddhist philosophy. Not all monasteries were focused on developing intellectual knowledge, some taught music, chanting, dance, rituals, and art.

The turmoil of the twentieth century had a devastating effect on Tibet's ancient Buddhist traditions. In the aftermath of the 1959 revolt, as many as 6,000 monasteries and nunneries were destroyed along with thousands of religious texts and artifacts. Monks and nuns were imprisoned or killed. A few thousand Buddhist monks managed to escape, bringing with them sacred texts and art. The first groups of monks were housed in Buxar Duar, a former British prisoner-of-war camp across the Bhutanese border in West Bengal. Historic photographs show

Monks pouring tea to serve for breakfast at the monastery.

the emaciated monks, teachers, and students, sitting outside crossed-legged, trying to restart monastic training. One of the Tibetans I met at Dharamsala said that when he escaped and saw how destitute everyone was, he felt he couldn't continue as a monk but needed to help the refugees. He derobed and became a cook in the refugee camp. Although his children have asked him and his wife to join them in the USA, he is happy where he is, in an apartment built on a cliff with a view of the Dalai Lama's rooftop. He said whenever His Holiness gives a talk, he can walk downhill and attend the teaching. He spends his days monk-like in study, meditation, and prayer.

Monks were given land near the settlements to rebuild their monasteries and to cultivate farmland. The three large teaching monasteries from the Gelug school which were in Lhasa—Sera, Ganden, and Drepung—were reestablished in the South India State of Karnataka. These monasteries were enormous and wealthy: Sera Monastery, the oldest of the three, founded in 1419, included nineteen hermitages and three colleges. It was known for its Great Assembly Hall. With nearly 5,000 monks, it was one of the largest in Lhasa. When the monastery was burned, 300 of the monks escaped in the 1960s and rebuilt their monastery in exile. Over time, the leading monks of all lineages have rebuilt their old monasteries throughout India and Nepal. These monastic communities have been providing teachings so that younger generations of monks have the knowledge and skills to preserve the sacred tradition.

The Dalai Lama explained the situations of the monks around the time of his escape.

> At that time, at least a few thousand monk students were already there. We made special arrangements so they could continue to study. Today in southern India, the big monastic institutions have been reestablished. About 10,000 monk students carry on the traditional way of studying.

Exile has changed the way monasteries operate. Without the traditional patronage from a government and a large population, the monasteries have had to find new ways for financial support. Some have sought international donors from individuals and institutions. Many of the monks regularly travel abroad to teach and perform cultural and religious rituals while others live abroad and continue to contribute to their monasteries in India, Nepal, and Bhutan.

The larger monasteries include up to a thousand people. There are now over 150 Tibetan monasteries in India and Nepal with a total population of between 25,000 and 35,000 monks and nuns, although not all of them are Tibetans. These monasteries are all reconstructions of the large ones abandoned or destroyed in Tibet. They are the custodians of Tibet's classical culture and knowledge.

His Holiness Chetsang Rinpoche is the head of the Drikung Kagyu school of Tibetan Buddhism.

The Dalai Lama is not the head of Tibetan Buddhism. Unlike the Catholic Pope, he has no power in the monasteries. The four main schools of Tibetan Buddhist tradition—Ningma, Gelug, Kagyu and Sakya—operate independently with their own monastic structures. However, the Dalai Lama's active engagement with modernity has influenced monasteries to broaden their education by including science and mathematics in their curricula. He has continuously emphasized the need to modernize, providing the monastic population with motivation to participate and engage with scientists. For example, the twenty-sixth Mind and Life Dialogue, which I will be discussing in greater detail later, was held in Drepung Monastery in Mundgod, Karnataka, India in 2013. They discussed the nature of reality, consciousness, and the human mind. In addition to an audience of 900 in the hall with the Dalai Lama and the scientists, 5,000 monks and nuns watched the conference on a screen in a larger hall. Two years later, the thirtieth Mind and Life Dialogue: Perception, Concepts, and Self took place at Sera Monastery. The Dalai Lama has not only helped reestablish key monasteries in India, but he has also modernized Tibetan Buddhism so it's more relevant in today's world. He was able to do this through his remarkable ability to inspire and motivate through his scholarship and deep understanding of Buddhism.

COMPASSION AT WORK

While traveling in Ladakh searching for nomads, we drove through vast open landscapes devoid of human activities until we suddenly encountered a monastery. Fortunately, the gate was open so we drove in. The driver went in to inquire about a place to spend the night and came out with a monk, who was shaking his head as he talked. I knew women weren't allowed to stay in monasteries. The problem was, it was dark, and there was nowhere else to go. Suddenly, monks hurriedly passed by with buckets full of water. One carried a broom. They cleaned a guest room which was still under construction to make a place for me to spend the night. There was a twin-size bed with a Tibetan rug on it, but I had my sleeping bag. I was grateful for the kindness shown to me. Even if a female cannot spend the night at a monastery, the compassion of the monks overruled the regulations. I can't help but think the Dalai Lama's effort to modernize the monastery was at play here.

This novice nun was carried out of Tibet in a basket.

PROMOTING NUNS' EDUCATION

The Dalai Lama's influence on the nuns has been even greater than his influence on the monks. But first, when did the nuns become refugees? Few Tibetan nuns escaped in the early years of exile. Most of the nuns escaped Tibet in the late 1980s. Delek Yangdong and several nuns living in East Tibet had decided to make a pilgrimage to Jokhang Monastery, considered the most sacred monastery in Tibet. It is in the center of Lhasa by the Potala Palace. Jokhang was built in 642 by King Songtsen Gampo, the first king of unified Tibet. The temple was boarded up during the Cultural Revolution in 1966, and for over a decade, worship was forbidden. In the 1980s the temple was restored and has become once again one of the most important places for Tibetan pilgrimages. Delek Yangdong and her group of travelers prostrated, to show reverence, from their village to Lhasa to visit the temple. I asked her to show me how she did this. She put her palms together over her head, brought them down to her heart, then put her hands on the ground and stretched so her whole body was flat on the ground. Then she got up and prostrated again from where her hands landed. What dedication! It took the party a year and a half to reach Lhasa in this fashion only to be told by the Chinese police to go to Mount Kailash first and stop by Jokhang on their way back to their village, as the temple was overcrowded with pilgrims. Mount Kailash is considered sacred among four religions—Buddhism, Hinduism, Bon, and Jainism—and is a pilgrimage site. When this party reached Mount Kailash, the group leader made known his plans to escape to India. Delek Yangdon and a few others decided to accompany him. Delek Yangdon described:

> I went with the group on the pilgrimage to Lhasa, and I was excited because I wanted to see Lhasa; all my life I had heard so much about it. We prostrated till Lhasa. Along the way, we never faced a problem, the guards would come and take Rinpoche aside and they would talk. For me the hardest part of the pilgrimage was during the monsoon. We would do prostrations in the rain and in the mud. Our clothes got wet and dirty, and we could not wash them out every day. We washed them when we could and on Sundays when we rested. We hoped they would dry fast. I got calluses on my elbows and knees. Some people wore pads on their elbows and knees to help protect

them, but I didn't. Sometimes I caught a cold but really, I was fine. I started my education on the pilgrimage. I started reading Tibetan and memorizing prayers. I had seven relatives in the group on the pilgrimage, so I never got homesick. Also, there were about forty to fifty nuns in the group, and we became friends and helped each other. The oldest person in the group was a layman who was fifty-one, and the youngest was a monk who was nine. Both stayed in Tibet and did not join the group who came to India.[5]

When they arrived in India, there was nowhere for the nuns to live since they could not live in the monasteries. She then joined a group of nuns in building Dolma Ling nunnery.

Exile provided new opportunities for nuns. Higher-level education for nuns was rarely available, resulting in an education gap between monks and nuns. The Dalai Lama urged the nuns to take up debating. The debating practices that

Nuns studying to attain a degree to become teachers.

nuns undertake daily, and the annual Jang Gönchoe inter-nunnery debate have been highly beneficial to nuns. Debating has expanded their understanding of Buddhist philosophical texts and allowed them to develop the debating skills that are tested during the Geshema exams. The Dalai Lama revised the nuns' course of study to include the seventeen year-long traditional monastic curriculums. The rigorous program of study is comprised of Buddhist philosophy, Tibetan language, the practice of debate, and training in ritual arts such as creating sand mandalas and butter sculptures. It also includes English, basic mathematics, science, and computer skills. They acquire self-sufficiency skills such as tofu making and handicrafts and manage the overall life of their nunnery. Upon graduation, the nuns receive the Geshema degree, equivalent to the Geshe degree for monks. In May 2016, twenty nuns received the Geshema degree for the first time in Buddhist history. The Tibetan Nuns Project and its supporters have also played a significant role in making this landmark achievement possible, working over the past twenty-five years to increase the educational level of nuns. Dolma Ling Nunnery became the first institute dedicated to providing higher Buddhist education for nuns.[6]

The opportunity to earn the Geshema degree has had the continuous support of the Dalai Lama, the Department of Religion and Culture of the Kasur Rinchen Khando, and the Central Tibetan Administration, along with the dedication of the nuns themselves. Samdhong Rinpoche explained that, in exile, opportunities for nuns have expanded; upon obtaining higher education, nuns are empowered to teach.

> *Now we have Geshema nuns. This is all new. We didn't have this in Tibet. At this moment there is a great need for nun teachers, so all the Geshema are going into teaching.*

Two years ago, the Dalai Lama attended a Long-Life Offering prayer (*tenshug*) presented to him by Buddhist nuns, including those from the ancient Bon religion. It was a historic event as it was the first time a tenshug was offered by nuns as well as being the first time tenshug has taken place at the Tsuglagkhang temple. Almost 900 nuns representing over forty nunneries in India, Nepal, and Bhutan offered the tenshug as a mark of gratitude for his continuous support for them. Standing on the platform near him, I could see how happy and proud he was. Afterall, he made it possible for the nuns to study for their Geshema degree.

The Dalai Lama in Tsuglagkhang Temple attending the Long Life prayer.

Novice nun in ordination ceremony conducted by the Dalai Lama.

ORDINATION CEREMONIES

I was invited to attend two ordination ceremonies at the Dalai Lama's private temple. One was for the monks and the other for novices. As I walked up the steep hill, snow-capped mountain peaks appeared now and then amidst the trees. The Dalai Lama's private temple suddenly materialized beyond a garden path. Although only a few minutes' walk from the bustling town of Dharamsala, the temple setting was so quiet, only the chirping of birds disrupted the stillness. The Dalai Lama's private temple is, by his design, modest. He may have wanted to set an example; regardless, this temple suits his personality.

The day I attended, sixty novice monk and nun candidates were sitting on their cushions in silence. When the Dalai Lama entered, the simple temple transformed into a sacred space. It felt as if he breathed life into the bronze statues and thangka paintings: Padmasambhava, Vajrasattva, Maitreya, and Tara. The three great protectors—Manjushri, manifestation of wisdom; Avalokiteshvara, manifestation of compassion, love, and altruism; and Vajrapani, manifestation of power and skill—were present for the ordination ceremony. When the Dalai Lama paid respect to a large painting of the Buddha above his throne, it was as if Sakyamuni Buddha was sitting there in person. He then walked over to the novices before commencing the elaborate ordination ceremony. The novices stood shyly and smiled as he walked up and down the rows greeting them. Once the ceremony began, the Dalai Lama took on a serious demeanor appropriate to the occasion—he was continuing the Buddhist monastic lineage that was established back in Tibet, in exile.

Towards the end of the ceremony, small groups of novices approached the Dalai Lama who sat cross-legged on his throne. He explained the significance of the Buddhist symbols—the robe, the sieve, and the alms bowl—to the novices. I was photographing from the back of the temple, trying not to intrude, when unexpectedly, pointing at a spot next to him, the Dalai Lama said, "You can stand next to me and photograph from here!" When I approached, I was moved to see the novices with their awestruck, glowing faces close to the Dalai Lama. I was told that it was unprecedented for anyone to be allowed on the platform, especially to stand next to his throne. Only the Dalai Lama is allowed to break protocol. How did he know I wanted to take that photograph? It is common knowledge the Dalai Lama has loved watches and all things mechanical from a young age. Less known is the fact that he photographed and printed his own work in Lhasa. Imagine that! A darkroom in Potala Palace. So, he was directing me on my photo shoot!

The Dalai Lama instructing monks near the end of the ordination ceremony.

The Dalai Lama addressing the newly ordained novices as he leaves his temple.

OLD AND NEW BUDDHISTS

When the Dalai Lama taught Nagarjuna's Commentary on Bodhicitta and Gyalsey Thokme Sangpo's third-seven Practices of a Bodhisattva at Bodh Gaya in 2018, one of the most important Buddhist pilgrimage sites, the place where the Buddha attained enlightenment, 30,000 people from seventy countries attended. His teaching was simultaneously translated and broadcasted into English, Chinese, Hindi, Russian, Mongolian, Vietnamese, Korean, Japanese, French, Spanish, Romanian, and the Amdo and Tawo Tibetan dialects. They represent what the Dalai Lama called "old and new Buddhists."

Addressing the audience, the Dalai Lama said there was a time when Tibetan Buddhism was dismissed as Lamaism. Tibet was so isolated that until the Dalai Lama presented at the World Fellowship of Buddhists in Sarnath, India in 1964, other Buddhists had misconceptions about Tibetan Buddhism—many of them thought it was Lamaism. The Dalai Lama's talk was well accepted, and they started to see that Tibetan Buddhism could be Buddhism. The Buddha taught in different ways, depending on the students, which evolved into different Buddhist traditions. However, all the teachings are based on the four noble truths and wisdom and compassion for all living beings. At the conference, the Dalai Lama said that if everyone raised the standard of his moral principles, happiness and peace could be achieved, and that the Buddhists of different countries should understand each other and put the teachings of the Lord Buddha into practice. Since then, Tibetans have been considered the custodians of the pure Nalanda Tradition. I would add here that the Dalai Lama, through his teachings and his books, has made Tibetan Buddhism more accessible and comprehensible to both Buddhists and non-Buddhists. The Dalai Lama explained:

> Today, Buddhism is being revived and we still have access to the writings of many great Mongolian masters. It was one of my debate assistants, Ngodrup Tsognyi, a Mongolian, who stimulated my interest in the Middle Way (Madhyamaka) School of Thought. Several hundred Mongolian monks are now studying in the monasteries in South Indian, and I've advised them how important it is that they keep up their studies.

*We also have here many people from the Himalayan region and
there are many monks and nuns from their communities in our
monasteries and nunneries. They have made up the numbers since
the flow of monks and nuns out of Tibet has declined; something
we can be mutually grateful for.*

*There are people here too who are not traditionally Buddhist,
who come from Judeo-Christian backgrounds. With improved
communications and travel facilities many more people have taken
an interest in Tibetan religion and culture, have offered us support,
and have been inspired by the teachings of the Buddha. You are
new Buddhists. We, old Buddhists of Tibet and the Himalayan
Region, bid you welcome.7*

Who exactly are the old and the new Buddhists? I was surprised to see mainly
youngsters from the Himalaya regions at the ordination ceremonies. When I met
Ven. Samdhong Rinpoche, I asked him why there were so many non-Tibetan
novices. He explained they are what the Dalai Lama referred to as Old Buddhist:

*The big monasteries left or destroyed in Tibet were reestablished by
the Tibetan refugees in India. In the beginning, these monasteries
only had Tibetan refugees. Nowadays, the Indian monk and nun
population is much larger than the Tibetan refugee population. The
Himalaya people, in the regions of Ladakh, Lahaul, Sikkim, Arunachal
Pradesh, Spiti, and Bhutan are traditionally Tibetan Buddhist
followers. Monks from these regions have joined the Tibetan
monasteries. We also have monks from Mongolia and Russia. In the
south, there are more than 600 Mongolian monks in the Tibetan
monasteries and nunneries. It will continue to increase. India has a
huge Himalaya region. In the past, before 1959, Buddhists from the
border regions used to go to Tibet and Nepal to study.*

For a while, monasteries have been thriving in exile due to the large influx of
Tibetan nuns and monks who escaped in the 1980s. Since then, it has been nearly
impossible for Tibetans to escape. As a result, there are now more monks and
nuns from the Himalaya regions than monks from Tibet in the Tibetan monasteries

in India. Prior to 1959, Buddhists from the Himalayan regions used to travel to the large Tibetans monasteries in Lhasa to study. With the revitalization of Tibetan monasteries and nunneries in India, it is not surprising to find monks and nuns from the Himalaya regions studying there. Historically, the three great monasteries of Lhasa served as centers of Buddhism for the Himalayan world. As I reflected on my experience photographing Buddhist ceremonies and traditions, I realized that history is repeating itself. It has come full circle.

Monks from the Himalaya regions bowing to the Dalai Lama during the ordination ceremony.

I was not expecting to find any Westerners at the ordination ceremonies. Again, I asked Ven. Samdhong Rinpoche. He said that when they first settled in Dharamsala, in the 1960s, there were many hippies seeking alternative belief systems. He said initially, they didn't pay attention to them as they appeared to be "shopping" around for an alternative religion to their own. To his amazement, some of them became scholars and teachers of Buddhism. Samdhong Rinpoche explained that the Dalai Lama refers to them as New Buddhists:

> In the beginning when we came in 1959, the Western people were in the hippie movement. They were interested in many kinds of religion, so they also came to Buddhism. We never took them seriously. But actually, many good Western professors were produced during this period, like Bob Thurman and Jeffrey Hopkins. There are many authentic scholars working in the academic field today. Lots of books have been translated, written, and published.

Ven. Samdhong Rinpoche explained that they did not expect Tibetan Buddhism to spread all over the world.

> I was just saying a few days ago, from 1959 until today, the Buddhism that has been preserved in Tibetan language and tradition has been distributed all over the world. We are not missionaries; we do not try to promote the Dharma. It is something unique that I cannot explain. Everywhere in the world—the Western world, Africa, Latin America, and Asia of course, where Buddhism is not new—people are drawn to Tibetan Buddhism. I don't think there is a single country without a center for Tibetan Buddhist study or a meditation center. Lots of Tibetan monks and teachers are going everywhere to teach. Lama Tubten Zupa and Lama Yeshi— none of them thought they would be good teachers for Westerners.

> People in the academic field are also interested. Universities have research centers of Tibetan Buddhist studies and comparative religious studies. Many books have been translated and written and published by non-Tibetan scholars.

As I said, Tibetans have neither the skills nor financial resources
to promote the Dharma. Its spread in the West was purely due to
people's interest.

While the Dalai Lama believes that people should stick to their own religion of birth and does not proselytize Buddhism, Tibetan lamas have spread all over the world. They have created meditation centers, temples, and monasteries near where Tibetans live and beyond. Even in the small town of 15,000 where I live, a highly accomplished Tibetan monk holds weekly practices and meditation sessions in his house as well as Buddhist teaching on a larger scale. None of the members of the *sanga* (Buddhist community) are Tibetans. Only one or two Tibetans live nearby, so he travels to the Tibetan community in Portland, Oregon and to Asia to teach. Khenpo Karten Rinpoche escaped from Tibet to Dharamsala in 1996 and has lived in the United States for over ten years. During the 2020 pandemic he has provided friendship to the elderly who are not able to visit their families. They sit outside in the garden, six feet apart, for tea and conversation.

The Dalai Lama explaining the significance of the begging bowl to western novices.

Rinpoche told me that when people tell him they are lonely, he tells them, "I am your family. When you feel lonely, come and I will make you tea." He smiled and added, "Just like the Dalai Lama, everyone is my brother or sister." Yes, the Dalai Lama works in quiet ways.

The Dalai Lama's attempt to preserve Tibetan Buddhism isn't reliant on the cult of his personality. Far from it. When the Dalai Lama finally visited the West, some of the Tibetan teachers who'd already had exposure in the West were nervous. They thought they would lose their followers to the Dalai Lama. He told them to continue teaching— as Kagyu, Ningma, Sakya. He is ingenious in that way. He doesn't have a big ego. Tibetan Buddhism has spread in the world today because it is relevant to our society. Tibetan culture exists today because it is resilient to changes. Its ability to survive is due to its rational scientific nature; it is not stuck in superstition or dogma. The Dalai Lama's effort to modernize Buddhism has succeeded.

The Dalai Lama's classical education and lifelong practice of Buddhism has shaped the way he views the world. He is the spiritual leader of the Tibetans who has taken "religion" out of Buddhism and made its philosophy and teaching accessible to us all. The Dalai Lama's push for modernization in the monastic population is a way to engage them in modernity. In nature, when a species cannot transform, it dies. The Dalai Lama knew the isolationist policy of Tibet ultimately nearly killed off its culture. Cultures often want to keep other people out. "Nobody can understand us therefore, nobody can be us," is a way to keep a culture "pure." But the Dalai Lama has a different approach. He has opened Tibetan culture to the world, and when the world caught a glimpse of this culture of compassion and peace, they wanted to be a part of it. In exile, the Dalai Lama and the Tibetan people have shown the world that embracing common core human values can create a happier world.

VISION FOR A BETTER WORLD: SPIRITUAL AND ETHICAL REVOLUTION

What is a spiritual revolution and how does spirituality differ from religion? Spirituality, the Dalai Lama tells us, is "concerned with the qualities of the human spirit—such as love and compassion, patience, tolerance, forgiveness, contentment, a sense of responsibility, and a sense of harmony—which bring happiness to both self and others."[8] He understands most of the world's population does not engage in traditional religious practice yet are interested in promoting positive qualities and nurturing inner values in their everyday lives. By focusing the revolution on spirituality based on innate, basic, universal values, he has invited everyone to join.

What does the Dalai Lama mean by ethical practices? He explains:

> *[since] love and compassion involve concern for others' well-being, it implies the people who have these qualities understand the potential impact of their own actions on others and conduct themselves accordingly. We cannot be loving and compassionate unless at the same time we curb our own harmful impulses and desires.*[9]

Furthermore, "ethical discipline is indispensable because it is how we mediate between the competing claims of my right to happiness and others' equal rights."[10] The Dalai Lama believes that ethics is universal; therefore, his appeal for an ethical revolution is based on principles that are held by many. He tells us, when an individual's overall state of heart and mind is wholesome, our actions themselves will be ethically wholesome. Spirituality and ethical practices go hand in hand!

The Dalai Lama's call for a spiritual and ethical revolution is fundamentally a call for a total reorientation, away from our habitual preoccupation with the self, and toward the wider community of beings. He asks us to develop our own compassion and recognize others' interests alongside our own. Our problems, such as war and violence which are experienced externally, and emotional and psychological sufferings which are experienced internally, simply cannot be solved if we continue living as we do. He is not naive to believe that the cultivation of spiritual and ethical values will alleviate all problems; however, when these dimensions are neglected, as they have been for centuries, there is absolutely no hope of achieving lasting peace and happiness. The Dalai Lama sees that many of the man-made problems stem from each of us caring for ourselves at the expense of others. We look out for our own profit, often by exploiting others. He tells us we need to change our relationship to each other—instead of competing to win, we need to learn to cooperate.

THE POWER OF COMPASSION AND LOVE

The Dalai Lama explains that from the moment of birth, we depend on others' compassion and love for our own survival. He often cites his mother as his first "guru." She was a very compassionate person who showed him affection and love, but her compassion also extended to people outside her family. Even with seven children, she treated all children as if they were her own. He remembers as a young child that she would share whatever food she had with hungry children who came to their house. The Dalai Lama says he would be a different person if he was not raised by such a compassionate person. He asks us to think beyond our own families, our own cities and countries and to embrace all humans. No doubt this feeling of compassion towards everyone came from his mother. When the Dalai Lama fled to India, all the Tibetan diaspora considered the Dalai Lama's mother as their mother.

He doesn't just tell us to be compassionate—he works at being compassionate. He cultivates a positive state of mind and the desire to be of service to others during his daily morning meditation sessions. By establishing a positive mindset, he says, there is then the possibility to be compassionate all day long. One day, when I went to his compound to attend an ordination ceremony, I saw him blessing a newborn child. I recognized the person who was holding the baby, so I went over to congratulate him. He told me that his daughter was sick, and though he and his wife were not Buddhist, they thought the Dalai Lama could heal her. This surprised me, as I recollected the Dalai Lama, on more than one occasion, warning us that despite people asking him to cure them of their illness, he has no magic powers with which to heal people. I've heard him say, gleefully, after an operation, "You see, if I have healing powers, I would have cured myself!" Having said that, the Dalai Lama still generously shares his abundant compassion.

When people ask for healing, he shows his concern by listening to their problems and sharing in their suffering. A little attention, a little kindness—most of the time that is all people need. This is the power of compassion.

Compassion and love are not luxuries, the Dalai Lama informs us; they are the source of inner and external peace and are fundamental to the survival of our species. They are the source of all spiritual qualities—of forgiveness, tolerance, and all the virtue. Compassion makes our lives meaningful and is the source of lasting happiness and joy.

CULTIVATING LASTING HAPPINESS AND INNER PEACE

The Dalai Lama says that everyone, regardless of country of origin, level of education and wealth, gender, age, or religion all desire to live a happy and peaceful life. While the main goal of life is happiness, our quest for happiness has failed because of our overemphasis on material gain. The Dalai Lama tells us the problem is not materialism but the erroneous assumption that enduring happiness can be generated from a series of experiences which gratifies the senses, such as pursuits of pleasure and leisure activities. These are short lived and give us temporary happiness. The prevalence of anxiety, stress, feelings of isolation and loneliness, uncertainty, and depression—all symptoms of self-absorption—indicates that we need more than material wealth to be happy.

Most of us don't think of happiness as a skill, but it is. And like all skills, it requires effort and time to develop. The Dalai Lama tells us that human beings, unlike animals, have the capacity to experience happiness at a deeper level. The source of lasting happiness is contingent on inner peace, and real inner peace depends on our mental attitude and our emotions. The Dalai Lama tells us that we have the potential to experience both positive and negative emotions, and it's up to each of us to decide which one we want to cultivate. Our emotional crises are caused by our hatred, anger, jealousy, envy, and other negative thoughts. To alleviate suffering, we will need to confront these negative thoughts and emotions and let go of our tendency to cling to our own needs at the expense of other people. The Dalai Lama tells us to relinquish our envy and let go of our desire to triumph over others. Instead, we should try to benefit others. However, if we cannot be of help to others, at least don't harm them.

UNIVERSAL RESPONSIBILITY

The essence of the Dalai Lama's teaching is universal responsibility, and he has been teaching how critical this is since he first started to travel globally. The Dalai Lama believes that "our every action has a universal dimension," and therefore it is "essential that we cultivate a sense of universal responsibility."[11] Nothing is outside of our concern. He explains that the benefit of developing a sense of universal responsibility is that we become sensitive to the needs of others, not just those who are close to us. We participate in the same global economy, and we live on the same planet. Changes in climate and environments affects us all. Since we are all interconnected, all our actions have global consequences. Nothing illustrates this concept of global interconnection more than the rapid spread of the global coronavirus pandemic in 2020, which spared no one and affected every one of us. There are people refusing to wear masks, citing their innate freedom to make individual decisions. The consequence of this self-centered behavior has only spread the pandemic further.

On a personal level, considering his position and apparent privilege, does this exceptional person identify with humanity at large? Asked if he gets lonely, the Dalai Lama replied, "If I think I am the only Dalai Lama in the world and I don't have a wife and I don't have children, I could get lonely." But of course, he doesn't think like that. He situates himself as one among many. He doesn't create a special position for himself. "If, when I meet people and think, I am a Tibetan, an Easterner, and a Buddhist, I only put a distance between myself and others. When I greet people as my fellow brothers and sisters, there is closeness."

EMBRACING EVERYONE AS HIS FAMILY

The Dalai Lama seems to have an innate feeling about the benefits of following the principles of democracy for people worldwide. For example, the Dalai Lama puts democracy into action even in small gatherings. I was one of about twenty people invited to attend a private dialogue between the Dalai Lama and three other Nobel Laureates—Shirin Ebadi, Iranian; Mairead Maguire, Northern Ireland; and American Jody Williams. It was held in his reception room. The moderator explained to the audience that we were to remain quiet "as if we weren't there." After almost an hour of discussion, the Dalai Lama turned to the audience and said, "Now it's your turn to ask questions." The moderator interrupted the Dalai Lama and told him that she was the only one who was allowed to ask questions. Laughing, he turned to his colleagues and said, "We are discussing global peace and we have a totalitarian situation here! Let's take a vote. Who is in favor of the audience asking us questions?" All three Nobel Laureates agreed with the Dalai Lama. He turned to the moderator and said, "Democracy has won!" and laughed some more. His laughter was not malicious. He had made a point and the laughter softened the situation. Not only were we acknowledged, but our voices were also encouraged and heard.

When his colleagues and the moderator left, the Dalai Lama came over to greet us. A few who knew him encircled him. After briefly talking with them, the Dalai Lama graciously moved to open up the circle to include all of us. Many people beamed, while some were moved to tears. I was extremely heartened by his simple and natural gesture. With a few small steps, he made us all feel a part of his family.

To make this vision for a better world a reality, the Dalai Lama advocates seeing ourselves as one of seven billion people living in one shared home—our planet. He says, "Living a truly ethical life in which we put the needs of others first, and provide for their happiness, has tremendous implications for our society. If we change internally—disarm ourselves by dealing constructively with our negative thoughts and emotions—we can literally change the whole world."[12]

The Dalai Lama invites us to consider ourselves a tourist to this world. "Could there really be anything to be gained from harming others during our stay here," he asks. "Is it not preferable, and more reasonable, to relax and enjoy ourselves quietly, just as if we were visiting a different neighborhood?" He implores us to "help in however small away those who are downtrodden and those, who, for whatever reason, cannot or do not help themselves." He bid us to "try not even to think of yourself as better than the humblest beggar" reminding us poignantly, "you will look the same in your grave."[13]

The Dalai Lama helps us see our past selfishness and shows us a path to living in harmony. He gives us the tools to tackle destructive emotions and to cultivate inner peace. He reminds us, "in addition to developing a sense of universal responsibility, we need actually to be responsible people."[14] His message has immediate relevance and importance today as the world's population continues to grow and natural resources suffer depletion. We are extremely fortunate that this is one special voice that speaks for a more compassionate, peaceful, and just world. In the time of COVID-19, we are all monks and nuns isolated in the "monastery" of our homes. The Dalai Lama's future vision is possible when we all have a bit of Tibetan in us.

The Dalai Lama mediating in his private home.

THE DALAI LAMA'S STORY: A GLOBAL LEADER

One day, when the Dalai Lama saw me outside of his private temple waiting for him to conduct one of the many ordinations, he came over and casually invited me to photograph him while he meditated. Many of his attendants had become quite friendly toward me, although from the perturbed manner by which one of the attendants greeted me as I was escorted to his meditation room, I had the impression this was a seldom-granted privilege. His personal residence is not large, and the room where he meditates is sparsely furnished. The focal point of the large room is the oversized stuffed chair. Two large LED lights, a statue of Buddha, and several gadgets are placed on the table in front of him. I couldn't tell if one of the gadgets was a radio, but he had said he listened to BBC news every morning when he was not traveling. A chair was placed far from where the Dalai Lama sat, cross legged in his armchair, deeply absorbed in meditation.

The Secretary who had escorted me told me not to disturb the Dalai Lama. He pointed to the chair, quite far from the Dalai Lama and told me to photograph from there. It was before sunrise and still very dark. As I was setting up my tripod, the Dalai Lama called to me and said, "First come here and say good morning." Then he said, "I see you need light," and switched on a ceiling light. When I approached him, he held up one *mala*, a strand of 108 prayer beads, and told me he had escaped with it. He then picked up a second mala and said, "This one is for you." I felt my heart skip and uttered a gasp. He had already presented me with a bronze Buddha and a Dharma Wheel. I felt overwhelmed. The Dalai Lama gave a small chuckle. Then he said, "You don't need to sit there. You can come as close to me as you want." Within seconds, he was absorbed in deep meditation.

Through the camera's viewfinder, one foot away from the Dalai Lama, I saw his expression change from quiet serenity to focused concentration. Even in silence, it is apparent his mind is reflecting and thinking. He has told us when he reflects on his emotions, he applies it to his life for his practice to move beyond an intellectual level and towards practical living. His body was still and silent. His presence was peaceful. Perhaps he was focused on his primary practice of Tonglen, which absorbs the suffering of others while projecting his own happiness. The Dalai Lama has told us his main practice begins when he wakes up. He shapes his mind by dedicating his body, speech, and mind to limitless sentient beings. He spends hours in contemplation and mind transformation to dissolve habitual egotism. He tries to make his life useful and of benefit to others. This remains with him the whole day. This, he has said, is one of his favorite daily prayers.

> *With the wish to free all beings*
> *I shall always go for refuge*
> *To the Buddha, Dharma, and Sangha,*
> *Until I reach full enlightenment*
>
> *Enthused by wisdom and compassion*
> *Today in the Buddha's presence*
> *I generate the mind for full awakening*
> *For the benefit of all sentient beings.*
>
> *As long as space remains,*
> *As long as sentient beings remain,*
> *Until then, may I too remain*
> *To dispel the miseries of the world.*

Witnessing the Dalai Lama meditating I saw, for the first time, how he sees himself—as a simple Buddhist monk. Nothing in this room shouts out Dalai Lama. He has said that in his dreams he is a monk: he has never dreamed he is the Dalai Lama. The spiritual leader of the Tibetans, Buddhist scholar and teacher, Nobel Peace Prize Laureate, scientist of the mind, prolific writer, advocate of nonviolence, proponent of universal responsibility, and champion of secular ethics is principally a monk; a monk who has taken the vows of celibacy, nonviolence, poverty, and spiritual honesty and lives the life of a monk. He has dedicated his life to helping others find inner peace. We are fortunate that the Dalai Lama identifies himself as one of the seven billion people on earth and works to alleviate the suffering of all.

As I gazed at the Dalai Lama, I realized that the people of the Tibetan diaspora reflect the Dalai Lama. Their acts of generosity in sharing with me what they have—a meal cooked by a nomad over a stove in a tent, hospitality from monks at an isolated monastery in the middle of a cold night, the last banana from a hermit living in a cave—and their contentment in their lives no matter how basic their living situation, nearly choked me up. More than ever, I wanted to share my experience and insight into the rich Tibetan culture of nonviolence, compassion, and kindness. Its value to the world is immense. The Tibetan people appear content with what they have. They don't chase materialistic wealth or any external wealth. There is a sense of inner calm which comes from knowing what is important and what is not. Tibetan people's contentment and success can be attributed to the Dalai Lama's leadership, especially on a global scale.

How did the Dalai Lama become a global leader, the reader may ask, and why is he considered a global leader? After all, he is a monk by training and commands neither country nor army. The Dalai Lama achieves global influence and reach in an uncommon way. He travels to learn from the world and to promote the cultivation of warm-heartedness and human values such as compassion and kindness which he considers universal and innate. Heads of states and organizations, scientists, those who attend his teachings and public talks, readers of his extensive writings either in print or online, and visitors to his home in Dharamsala feel the effect of his infinite compassion and kindness, and in turn, they discover the compassion and kindness within themselves. This role was predicted, as a matter of fact, by the protector oracle of the Dalai Lamas, the Nechung Oracle. But the Dalai Lama understood his prediction wrong at first. When the Nechung Oracle predicted, while in Tibet, that the Dalai Lama would "shine" in the West, he interpreted "West" to mean India. He did not know then that, soon, he would go into exile, followed by 85,000 Tibetans, and on his eighty-fifth birthday he would have been in exile for sixty-one years without having set foot in Tibet. He also didn't know that by advocating a non-violent solution to the Tibet problem, he would be awarded the Nobel Peace Prize. This recognition and his collaboration with scientists would thrust him onto the world's stage where he would become a leading voice of compassion, wisdom, non-violence, and peace in a troubled world.

DEVELOPING GLOBAL RESPONSIBILITY

How did it all begin? The Dalai Lama is someone who sees the silver lining even in the darkest cloud. He lost his country at the age of sixteen and became a refugee at twenty-four and has faced many difficulties. He said that although being a refugee is unfortunate, it has given him opportunities to visit many countries and meet with religious and political leaders, scientists, businesspeople, scholars, and others who have enriched his awareness and understanding of the world, given him new insight, and helped broaden his mind. Had he remained in Lhasa, his life would have been more orthodox, and his days filled with ceremonies and "superficial" activities.

The Dalai Lama had traveled extensively in Asia but had not been to the West until he was thirty-eight years old. In 1973, he spent six weeks visiting Europe. As he was largely unknown on the world scene, he could walk around and meet people naturally, without causing a commotion. Coming from Tibet, a country that is materially poor, then being a refugee, he thought that material wealth would have helped people get further towards achieving happiness. Instead, he found the achievements in science and technology and the material prosperity resulting from such advances didn't translate into overall high levels of serenity and satisfaction. Instead, what he found was the paradox of external comfort coupled with internal psychological and emotional suffering. This visit planted the seed of thinking of himself as a citizen of the world rather than a simple monk living in a remote village in India. It ultimately changed how he saw his life's work. Perhaps his training and study could provide guidance to others. The Dalai Lama explained:

> In 1973, I first visited a few countries in Europe—UK, Germany, Switzerland, Norway, and Italy. I met many students and a wide range of people. I observed their lifestyles. They were materially advanced but there was a big question as to how much peace of mind they had. When I returned to Dharamsala, I felt that a materialistic life was no guarantee of a happy and peaceful mind. So, I started to develop a sense of global responsibility.

The Dalai Lama wanted to travel to the USA, but his visa application was blocked. President Nixon had visited China in 1972 and was seeking normalcy

in the US's relationship with China. Robert Thurman, professor of Indo-Tibetan Buddhist Studies at Columbia University, who was the Dalai Lama's first Western student in the sixties and one of the few who studied privately with His Holiness, said that the Dalai Lama then went into retreat, deep meditation, and studies.

> In a way, Henry Kissinger did him a favor. He didn't start all this responsibility of touring and teaching. He was sort of forced to stay more or less here (in India) with a little side trip to Europe and Thailand through the 70s and therefore he did retreats and important meditations and deepening studies.

According to Thurman, when he first met the Dalai Lama, he wasn't the charismatic person we know him now. His transformation became apparent when he reemerged from his retreat.

> I experienced him from then on as a really powerful guru teacher. He was ready to roll. He was less nervous. He was more self-confident. I believe he had some profound sunyata (aspect of Buddhist philosophy) type experience on his own, not just from his former life. His philosophical acumen and ability to explain was incredibly sharp. The big change I saw in His Holiness at that time was that he was super-hot to answer any dharma questions.

The Dalai Lama finally visited the USA in 1979 when Jimmy Carter was president. In his travels, the Dalai Lama observed and exchanged ideas, especially with scientists. Before these travels, his interest and commitment focused on the Tibetans. He explained:

> In 1979 I went to America. Since my childhood, I have had interests in science. I had meetings with scientists and further developed my interest. After I met with scientists, I thought the knowledge we kept for thousands of years may have value in today's world and that there is potential in sharing how to develop inner peace. With that motivation, we gradually developed serious discussion with scientists. Until that time, my main concern was to preserve our ancient knowledge.

As a newcomer to modernity, it must have been a shock when the Dalai Lama first encountered the Western world. In his travels, he observed that when he arrives in a new country, people are friendly, and everything seems pleasant. However, he soon learns that underneath the surface, many feel dissatisfied or unhappy with their lives. They tell him about their feelings of isolation and depression. He was at first surprised to discover that even people who live in countries where there is freedom and prosperity experience suffering and adversity. Reflecting on his own situation, he believes he was able to cope reasonably well due to his study and practice of developing inner peace through the cultivation of love, compassion, peace, and happiness, which enabled him to transform his despair. Had he been overwhelmed by anxiety; he would have not been able to cope with the situation and help the Tibetan refugees. From his own experience, he feels that the ancient knowledge of the mind and emotions, and the practice of training the mind to tackle disturbing emotions and to ultimately develop inner peace could be of potential benefit to all humanity. He explained:

> Nowadays we face tremendous amounts of emotional stress. We need more information about the mind and emotions. We can share with seven billion human beings how to achieve peace of mind by caring about individuals, families, and communities. We are fully convinced we can make contributions by reviving the ancient Indian understanding of the mind and emotions, reason, and logic.

The Dalai Lama is pragmatic, and he has a mission. Through his dialogue with scientists, he hopes to integrate contemporary science and science of the mind and, in doing so, an alternative way to promote physical and mental well-being.

SCIENTIST OF THE HEART AND MIND

The Dalai Lama's nearly forty years of interchange with scientists has had extraordinary outcomes. It began with his lifelong interest in science which led him to seek meetings with scientists—even when warned by his friend that discussions with scientists may lead him to disbelief in Buddhism. Hearing this, the Dalai Lama reflected that Buddhism has a long tradition of investigating the nature of the mind through meditation and analysis. He concluded not only that there was no risk, but that Buddha himself was an ancient scientist. He explained:

> Then I reflected on Buddha's own words—that it is important to experiment and investigate. I decided there wasn't much risk. I truly believe Buddhism is the investigation of reality and its explanation. Buddha himself mentioned, "Oh my follower monks and scholars, you should not accept my teachings out of faith, but rather through investigation and experimentation." One aspect of Buddha is that he is a great thinker; another aspect is that he is an ancient Indian scientist who emphasizes reasoning, not faith. I consider Buddha to be an ancient Indian scientist.

The Dalai Lama is at heart, a scientist. He is incredibly curious, and he is always wondering about why things happen and asking questions. He has often said that if he weren't a monk, he would be a scientist. The Dalai Lama in fact studied science with some of the greatest scientists. One of his first teachers was the German quantum physicist and philosopher Carl von Weizsäcker, with whom he had formal tutorials and, on many occasions, intensive workshops on quantum physics and its philosophical implications.[15] Another scientist whom the Dalai Lama encountered was David Bohm, a theoretical physicist who contributed to quantum theory, neuropsychology, and the philosophy of the mind. He credits his long discussions with Bohm over the course of two decades of contributing to his thinking about the way in which Buddhist methods of inquiry may relate to those used in modern science. The Dalai Lama felt that collaborating with scientists would have mutual benefits.

When I listen to Westerners talk about psychology, I feel their knowledge looks to be on the kindergarten level. The ancient Indian knowledge of psychology and emotions is highly developed. Scientists can learn from Buddhist, particularly about emotions and the mind—these things. In the meantime, our monk students should not be totally orthodox. They need to be more open minded and study science.

His Holiness' high regard towards science grew into an interest in working with scientists. What began as an intimate conversation in 1983 between Adam Engle, an American social entrepreneur, Francisco J. Varela, Director of Research at the CNRS (Centre National De Recherche Scientifique, France), a Chilean biologist, philosopher, and Buddhist practitioner, and the Dalai Lama evolved into the foundation of the first Mind and Life Dialogue in 1987. All three men believed that while scientists and Buddhists have different methodologies, they both seek to investigate the true nature of reality for the purpose of improving the quality of life for humanity. The Dalai Lama fondly recalled his first meeting with Francisco Varela.

My meeting with scientists (Mind and Life Dialogue) is over thirty years old. I first met with Francisco Varela who is a follower of Buddhism. During our discussion, I think in this very room, he mentioned that when he talks about science, his head is a scientist. When he talks about Buddhism, he says he dons a Buddhist cap. I also do that now. These days I describe myself as a half Buddhist monk, half scientist.

The Mind and Life Dialogues wouldn't have begun without the Dalai Lama's active participation and his generous support. His temple in Dharamsala provided a safe and intimate space where people gathered and ideas were brought forth and exchanged, incubated, researched, and ultimately implemented. The Dalai Lama Foundation enabled monks and nuns to attend these sessions.

The Dalai Lama's subtle leadership influenced the direction of the Mind and Life Institute. Initially focused on philosophical debates and the exchange of ideas, the Dalai Lama felt that they needed to move beyond dialogue into research and implementation. During the ninth session, he asked for rigorous scientific research on the effect of meditation on the brain and provided scientists with access to monks to conduct their research. Neuroscientist Richard Davidson took up the challenge. In his pioneer research, he used state of the art brain-imaging technology to study the long-term effect of meditation on the brain of meditators who have devoted 10,000–50,000 hours to meditation on compassion and awareness. Many other universities also began researching meditation. These studies proved the positive effects of meditation on achieving emotional balance. Before this research, neuroscientists believed that a person was born with a set number of neurons and experiences did not increase this number. Through this breakthrough research, scientists have now proven that the brain can be trained and physically modified. Davidson explained the meaning of neuroplasticity.

> It simply means that the brain changes in response to experience and in response to training. … we can take more responsibility for our own brains by cultivating healthy habits of mind. This is really the key discovery. And it's kind of amazing that when we nurture our minds in a healthy way, it turns out our brains change, and our brains change both functionally and structurally in ways that support enduring well-being.[16]

Science has now proven what contemplative practitioners have always known—basic human qualities such as mindfulness can be cultivated through meditative practices. Furthermore, mental training such as meditation can actually change the brain.

The Dalai Lama's ability to touch people's hearts by engaging with them has often had a transformative effect on people. As a real-life example of the power of compassion, the Dalai Lama's compassion helped establish a connection with Paul Ekman, Professor of Psychology at the University of California, San Francisco, a pioneer in the study of emotions and their relation to facial expression. During the tenth Mind and Life Dialogue, Ekman was so invigorated and inspired by his brief private exchange with the Dalai Lama during a tea break, instead of winding down his research as he had planned, he responded enthusiastically to the Dalai Lama's request for research on the secular version of meditation. Upon informing the Dalai Lama that he and several colleagues had developed a research project that combined Eastern meditative practices with Western psychological techniques, the Dalai Lama astounded him with a $50,000 grant from his book royalties to support the research. Cultivating Emotional Balance became the first

large-scale research project conducted by the Mind and Life Institute. Ekman was so affected by this encounter with the Dalai Lama that he went on to investigate the transformative quality of interactions with extraordinary people. The Dalai Lama asked Paul Ekman, who had advised the creators of Pixar's *Inside Out* (an animated film set inside a girl's head) to develop the Atlas of Emotions, an interactive tool created from the psychological study of emotion to help people navigate the quagmire of their feelings to attain peace and happiness.

The eleventh session of the Mind and Life Dialogue, held in 2003 at the McGovern Institute for Brain Research at the Massachusetts Institute of Technology (MIT), was a major turning point for the Mind and Life Institute as it was open, for the first time, to a public audience. Twelve hundred scientists, academics, journalists, Buddhist practitioners, Hollywood celebrities, and general public attended, with another thousand on the waiting list. At that time, Buddhism was not widely known to Western scientists; therefore, the idea of the two traditions collaborating to learn about the nature of the mind was still mind-boggling for many. MIT President Charles Vest introduced the session by welcoming the collaboration.

Recent scientific advances in the study of the brain and mind build on the rapidly accelerating progress in a broad range of disciplines … But at the most profound level these studies challenge those of us in the science and technologies to go still further afield, to grapple with insights and challenges from the world's great philosophical and spiritual tradition.

That is why this conference is important. It brings together scientists, academics, and Buddhist scholar-practitioners, all distinguished in their own fields, to explore topics of common concern in the spirit of open, honest inquiry that is the essence of the university.[17]

The dialogue's success led to numerous public dialogues being held in universities in the United States, Europe, Australia, and India. In 2005, the Dalai Lama was invited to speak at the 35th annual meeting of the Society for Neuroscience at the Washington Convention Center to an audience of 14,000. In the same year he published, *The Universe is a Single Atom: The Convergence of Science and Spirituality*. In 2018, Volume 1 of *Science and Philosophy in the Indian Buddhist Classic* was published.

Some of the world's greatest scientific and spiritual thinkers have collaborated and enriched the Mind and Life Dialogues, which have been held every two years. In addition to the publication of a book from each of the sessions, several significant outcomes have resulted from these collaborations. The Dalai Lama has introduced science into the traditional monastic education. Although changes in monastic education haven't happened for thousands of years, and many traditional senior monks had initial reservations, the Dalai Lama doesn't see this as radical, but as a matter of updating the curriculum. The Dalai Lama isn't just paying lip service to science but has said, "If science proves facts that conflict with Buddhist understanding, Buddhism must change accordingly. We should always adopt a view that accords with the facts." In ancient Buddhist cosmology, the universe was seen as flat with Mount Meru, a sacred mountain, at its center. The Dalai Lama explained that Buddhists must accept scientific reality and update their way of thinking. He explained:

> One casualty is Mt Meru. I don't believe in Mt. Meru. Modern scientific explanations of cosmology make it clear that Mt. Meru doesn't exist as the axis of the Universe. For example, there were senior monks who, at the beginning, had reservations. They thought their faith might be damaged. But I insisted. Now they accept the study of science as being very useful. In Southern India some of the larger monastic universities already have science programs.

In turn, science has benefited immensely from this unlikely collaboration. The Dalai Lama brings a Tibetan Buddhist perspective to the discussion—it exposes the scientist to the insights of Buddhist philosophy which has explored the inner workings of the mind for centuries. Tibetan Buddhist monks have rigorously scrutinized the mind through meditation in monastic universities in Tibet and now in India and Nepal. Initially, some of the scientists had been skeptical of using the mind to investigate itself. Over time, with specific research involving measurable hypotheses and experiments, the Dalai Lama has inspired a new generation of scientists to value first-person methods of scientific inquiry. Buddhist monks have been probing the depth of awareness that Western scientists, particularly psychologists, had not previously considered. The Dalai Lama asked Richie Davidson to take practices from Buddhism, turn them into secular form, and investigate their value through the tools of modern science. And, if he finds it useful, to disseminate them. One of the major findings is that wellbeing can be cultivated, something the Dalai Lama has always known and spoken about. The four pillars of wellbeing are informed by contemplative traditions and modern science. For Davidson, this "assignment" from the Dalai Lama has changed his life's work. He is committed to this work for the rest of his life.

This partnership with scientists has increased the legitimacy of practices based in Tibetan Buddhism in the eyes of the world. Buddhist meditation—outside of those who were practitioners—was uncommon thirty years ago. Science has validated that meditation can help the body and change the brain. Now mindfulness, meditation, loving kindness, and compassion are commonplace terms and concepts that have entered everyday culture and are integrated in our lives, businesses, schools, and hospitals. Science became a doorway through which the Dalai Lama extended his reach and influence, inviting a wider audience into joining the conversation. People who may not have been particularly interested in Buddhism have discovered the "science of the mind," (as the Dalai Lama sometimes refers to Buddhism) which offers them new ways of looking at themselves without the need to be a Buddhist.

The Dalai Lama has two goals when engaging with scientists. First, although science's advance in the physical world has been impressive, there are domains of reality that lie outside of scientific knowledge. The Dalai Lama's goal is to help make the current field of psychology more complete by providing a more expanded and detailed understanding of the mind. His second goal is to ensure that science serves humanity on more than just a physical level. He believes that if society were to pay more attention to the science of the mind and if science were to engage more with societal concerns, it would lead to "great advancement and novel outcomes." He believes science should never be divorced from the values that are important to the flourishing of human society.

The Dalai Lama believes that scientific and spiritual inquiry are different but complementary approaches of seeking truth. Ultimately, both are interested in understanding the nature of reality. He explained that scientific knowledge is incomplete. "Many aspects of reality, as well as some key elements of human existence, such as the ability to distinguish between good and evil, spirituality, artistic creativity—inevitably fall outside the scope of the method."[18]The dialogue between the two disciplines may develop to better service humanity. The Dalai Lama warns us that the world has witnessed tragedies caused by science and technology as well as religion.

His plea to us:

bring our spirituality, the full richness and simple wholesomeness of our basic human values, to bear upon the course of science and the direction of technology in human society. In essence, science and spirituality … share the same end, which is the betterment of humanity. … At its best, science is motivated by a quest for understanding to help lead us to greater flourishing and happiness. … Similarly, spirituality is a human journey into our internal resources, with the aim of understanding who we are in the deepest sense and of discovering how to live according to the highest possible idea. This too is the union of wisdom and compassion.[19]

THE 33RD MIND AND LIFE DIALOGUE

The Dalai Lama had wanted me to attend the 33rd Dialogue, which was focused on educating children to be compassionate, caring citizens committed to the common good. I knew that education was close to his heart and very important for him, so I rearranged my travel plans.

The versatile Tsuglagkhang Temple, where I had witnessed the Dalai Lama's New Year teaching and the Long-Life Ceremony in earlier weeks, had been transformed into a reception room of sorts to give it a friendly and intimate atmosphere. The presenters and moderators were seated around a rectangular table with the Dalai Lama at the head. More than 200 academics, educators, psychologists, scientists, monks, and nuns were seated in rows behind the presenters. Chairs were placed outside of the temple with large video screens to allow people to observe the session. There were sixteen presentations on the topic of childhood development, critical life skills that children acquire from social and emotional learning (SEL), application of SEL in the classrooms, and secular ethics.

The Dalai Lama's friendly informality set the tone for the five-day session. His hearty laughter often punctured the serious milieu, creating a sense of fun and enthusiasm. An open window provided access to members of the press to photograph and videotape. To photograph the Dalai Lama without the obstruction of people's heads, I had to hold my camera above my head. A photograph showing everyone laughing, including me holding up my camera above my head, made it to the Dalai Lama's website! What struck me is how open everyone was to debate and exploration. They weren't trying to win a point or to influence. Everyone was willing to see another viewpoint. Watching him interact with the presenters gave me further insight into the way the Dalai Lama influences people. Almost all the presenters spoke directly to the Dalai Lama—obviously, they sought his counsel. He listened attentively, at times leaning over to Thupten Jinpa, Buddhist scholar and principal English language translator for the Dalai Lama, if he didn't understand a point. I frequently observed people defer to him. However, His Holiness knows how to affirm, put people at ease and thus empower them. He shows his interest by listening with his whole heart and mind, often asking questions, or debating a point. When the speakers asked him for his input, he would tell them,

"You did this wonderful work," and would synthesize and summarize the key points. He would often add, "Very good!" The presenters would sit a little taller and smile from their heart.

When building the Tibetans schools in India, the Dalai Lama inspired individuals who then became passionate and engaged other people, until so many were on board to enable change to happen at a broader level. Similarly, the Mind and Life Dialogues started with three people having a conversation, then grew into an incubator for discovery in all the many fields this new science touches. This is the magic of the Dalai Lama's leadership. It starts with his vision, which transforms into a shared vision when others become engaged; these people then incorporate that vision into their work or use it as the basis for new work and expand exponentially.

PRAGMATIC LEADER

The first time I attended a public talk by the Dalai Lama was thirteen years ago in Switzerland. Reflecting on this now, I realized that he has been tirelessly and consistently reminding us of our own humanity just by being who he is. He has always said he is a human being first, and the Dalai Lama is his job description. He has been steadfast in showing us the power and honor associated with being a human. He is a model of what a human being can be.

The Dalai Lama has an uncanny ability to touch each of us individually and make us feel that he understands us and, by doing so, validates our worth. He taps into our universal urge to do something of value in our lives. He tells us if we all act now for a better future, we can make a difference. Because we believe in him, we believe in ourselves. The Dalai Lama has that mirroring effect on us. The Dalai Lama believes that change happens when each of us makes a positive contribution. Change comes through action; he often tells us. If we change and others change, then together we will make a difference.

I started attending the Dalai Lama's teachings, reading his books, and photographing the Tibetans diaspora on behalf of The Tibet Fund about the same time I was engaged by a European organization to develop a leadership and team building program. No doubt there are questions: how can a Tibetan monk—albeit the Dalai Lama, no matter how much he identifies himself as a fellow human being—be a model for a good leader? The Dalai Lama presents a viable alternative leadership style. Under his leadership, the Tibetan diaspora have built sustainable and prosperous communities over six decades in exile. The United Nations have cited the Tibetan refugee communities as model refugee communities. Tibetan culture has been preserved over three generations. The Dalai Lama has successfully introduced modernity to the ancient Tibetan culture. He has successfully democratized the exiled community with the introduction of a constitution and elected political leader. He has created schools for the Tibetan children steeped in Tibetan culture. He has modernized the monastic education by introducing mathematics and science, and he has sponsored the nuns so that they too can acquire the highest level of Buddhist education on par with the monks. Monastic populations have increased in India and, once again, monks and nuns from the Himalaya regions are studying together.

How did he help foster this success? The Dalai Lama didn't study being a leader in the modern world nor did he develop a grand strategy and present his agenda through a PowerPoint presentation. The Dalai Lama came to develop his ideas organically. He learned on a small scale from experts in their fields and from observing his people, then contemplating before disseminating his ideas. Those who were exposed to his ideas took these ideas, added some of their own and put them into action. The Dalai Lama doesn't have a big ego—he allows people to have their own voice. Critically, he doesn't need to see immediate results and gives people time to think and to experiment. His alternative approach to leadership allows people time and space to be creative and to bring their own ideas to the table. He trusts they will get there. This is a very powerful way to lead.

After successfully leading the Tibetan diaspora to their phenomenal accomplishments, he could have faded away. But that didn't happen. He has a grand global design—he is not bound by generation, nor does he focus on one group of people—he makes it universal. The Dalia Lama's tangible accomplishments as a global leader are equally robust. We witness the same leadership style in his role as a global leader. He tirelessly devotes himself to helping us through his teachings. But he always tells us we must find our own way. He gives us space to explore and to make mistakes. He trusts us that we will figure out how to live a life of enduring happiness.

The Dalai Lama's resilience and his profound trust in humanity to embrace universal responsibility and global peace is exemplary. But he is a realist and so he engages us to educate children to be good people so they can create the world that we have yet to create. The Dalai Lama has long been talking about the Buddhist principles of compassion, kindness, morality, and ethics and the value they add to the world. Slowly these ideas have permeated. How far can one man sway the entire world? Even a slight shift in the right direction is enormous.

The Dalai Lama's ideas on leadership have inspired me and His Holiness has served as a role-model for me professionally. When I helped design a program meant to bring out the potential of a company's leadership, I kept in mind his words: "we are part of seven billion people and are all interconnected. The success of any organization requires effective operation and teamwork at every level." I also applied the Buddhist theory of mental transformation to my work. The theory states that there are three levels of understanding: understanding through hearing and learning, understanding through critical reflection, and understanding through internalization. Leaning on all these principals, I was able to achieve the goal set before me professionally, and I have the Dalai Lama to thank for it.

VISIONARY LEADER

The Dalai Lama has dedicated his life to promoting peace and non-violence and was awarded the Nobel Peace Prize in 1989 for his endeavor. In his acceptance speech, he paid tribute to the man who founded the modern tradition of nonviolent action for change—Mahatma Gandhi, whom he credits for inspiring him. He accepted the prize:

> on behalf of the oppressed everywhere and for all those who struggle for freedom and work for world peace [and] on behalf of the six million Tibetan people, my brave countrymen and women inside Tibet, who have suffered and continue to suffer so much. They confront a calculated and systematic strategy aimed at the destruction of their national and cultural identities. The prize reaffirms our conviction that with truth, courage and determination as our weapons, Tibet will be liberated.

Asked how he felt about winning this prestigious award, the Dalai Lama replied that it doesn't mean anything for himself; however, he is pleased for the people who wanted him to win the award. He explained:

> When I received my first announcement, I was in the USA. Some media people wanted to meet me. I said this prize is nothing to me. I am just a simple Buddhist monk, no more, no less. I consider this prize a recognition of my contribution to peace.

When the Dalai Lama said this, I didn't get a sense that he was trying to be humble. I felt he genuinely doesn't care for accolades. Then he laughed and added:

> Bishop Tutu told me, before the Peace Prize, it is difficult to go to the White House. After the Prize, it is much easier to visit such a place.

Tibetans told me that before winning the Nobel Prize, His Holiness walked about freely in Dharamsala. Even when he traveled overseas, the media didn't bother him; they simply didn't know who he was. Winning the Nobel Prize changed all that. It certainly expanded his global reach.

The smiling face of the Dalai Lama has graced so many books and magazine covers that he is familiar to us. To start with, when he relinquished his political authority in 2011, he effectively ended a 400-year-old tradition in which the Dalai Lama serves as political and religious head of Tibet. Since then, he has had no political power and is not constrained by politics. As a result, his concern extends to all of humanity rather than being limited to a specific country.

The "simple monk" is without a country and lives as a refugee in a remote, hard to get to hillside city at the edge of the Himalayas in India. After a decade of helping settle the exile community in various parts of India, building schools and attempting to preserve Tibetan culture, the Dalai Lama began his global travels. He has dedicated the rest of his life to three main commitments: 1) to encourage people to be happy by helping them to understand that the basic human values of compassion and love are two necessities in life; 2) to support interreligious understanding and harmony; and 3) to promote the preservation of Tibetan language and culture and the protection of Tibet's natural environment. Unlike the majority of the world's leaders, his focal point isn't the next year or election cycle but encompasses the well-being of future generations. He understands that change takes time and believes that he won't be alive to see the fruit of the changes he promotes.

He is wholeheartedly dedicated to using his mind and speech to help others achieve happiness and eliminate suffering. "Helping others to develop inner peace," he says, "gives me great satisfaction, inner strengths, and meaning to my life. This is my primary commitment for the rest of my life." He does not seek followers; nonetheless, people seek him. His books are bestsellers, and thousands travel to attend his teachings; tickets to his teachings are routinely sold out within minutes.

The Dalai Lama has emerged as a highly respected and loved global leader. He has a compelling vision for humanity—he proposes nothing less than a revolution—although not a political, an economical, or even an uprising. "None of those external approaches have solved the world's problems," he explains, "the great movements of the last hundred years and more—democracy, liberalism, socialism—have all failed to deliver the universal benefits they were supposed to provide, despite many wonderful ideas." The Dalai Lama offers a vision for humanity in which the different approaches to understanding ourselves, each other, and our world can be integrated in a way we all benefit. He proposes an alternative approach—a spiritual and ethical revolution. This revolution starts deep within us.

ETHICAL LEADER

Although the Dalai Lama says that individuals need to take responsibility for change in order for the world to become kinder and a more peaceful place, he also believes individual governments need to solve some of the problems in the world. Besides asking us to dig deeper into our minds to master our own selves, he has been advocating changes in institutions—education, our natural environment, interreligious harmony, and peace and disarmament—which he says needs to be addressed by larger institutions of power so that the changes will continue.

EDUCATING FUTURE GENERATIONS

The Dalai Lama has always championed education for children. When the Tibetan diaspora first arrived in India, he took care of the children first, by asking his sister to build schools. The Dalai Lama believes that children hold the key to a more peaceful, kinder, egalitarian world. Modern education, the Dalai Lama believes, is too oriented towards how to achieve material well-being. We cannot fault children who have had twelve to fifteen years of training limited to material well-being and the concept that competition and winning are what matters, while failing to address the education of the heart and the exploration of inner values. To create a more compassionate world, education must be reoriented to show children the needs and rights of others as well as developing warm heartedness and compassion. The result of integrating the principles of nonviolence and peaceful conflict resolution at school, the Dalai Lama believes, is that children will be more aware of their feelings and emotions and feel a greater sense of responsibility both toward themselves and toward the wider world. To live a truly ethical life we need to start with children: education must open children's eyes to the needs and rights of others, and furthermore, they need to learn that their actions have a universal dimension.

The Dalai Lama believes that to truly reimagine human flourishing, children need to transform the values and attitudes they hold towards each other so that compassion and loving kindness form the basis for all their interactions and that the children accept and embrace their roles as local and global citizens. The Dalai Lama is a believer in the power of the individual and a cheerleader for children

Tibetan children start the day praying for loving kindness and peace for all.

who, as the next generation, have the potential to realize the benefits and fulfill the responsibilities related to the interdependence of humanity.

OUR NATURAL ENVIRONMENT

The Dalai Lama is one of the earliest leaders to advocate environmental protection. In fact, his citation for the 1989 Nobel peace prize states this:

> *The Dalai Lama has developed his philosophy of peace from a great reverence for all things living and upon the concept of universal responsibility embracing all mankind as well as nature. In the opinion of the Committee the Dalai Lama has come forward with constructive and forward-looking proposals for the solution of international conflicts, human rights issues, and global environmental problems.*

The Dalai Lama has been a strong advocate for treating the environment with respect and has framed the environmental movement as part of our universal responsibility. In his autobiography he states, "As a boy studying Buddhism, I was taught the importance of a caring attitude toward the environment." He brings the Buddhist approach of interdependence into his framework. "Although we do not believe that trees or flowers have minds, we treat them also with respect. Thus, we share a sense of universal responsibility for both mankind and nature." The Dalai Lama believes that nature is an integral part of the web of life, whereas we tend to see nature as a resource, separate from ourselves.

Since the early years of exile, the Dalai Lama has taken an interest in environmental issues, introducing ecology to the children. I've photographed many Earth Day field trips where students collect trash thrown in the forest and hills. The Dalai Lama's love of nature stems from his childhood.

> *My chief memory of the three-month journey across Tibet from my birthplace at Takster in the east to Lhasa, where I was formally proclaimed Dalai Lama as a four-year-old boy, is of the wildlife we encountered along the way. Immense herds of kiang (Tibetan wild ass) and drong (wild yak) freely roamed the great plains. Occasionally we would catch sight of shimmering herds of gowa*

*(the shy Tibetan gazelle), of wa, the white-lipped deer, or of tso,
our majestic antelope. I remember, too, my fascination for the
little chibi, or pica, which would congregate on grassy areas. They
were so friendly. I loved to watch the birds, the dignified gho, (the
bearded eagle) soaring high above monasteries perched up in the
mountains, the flocks of nangbar, (geese), and occasionally, at night,
to hear the call of the wookpa, (the long-eared owl).*[20]

The delightful description of the young boy's journey that would transform his life forever gives us a glimpse into what he found joyful. Sadly, the Tibet imprinted in his memory is no longer—every Tibetan he has spoken to reported on the absence of wildlife and the devastation of Tibet's forests. This is of major concern not only for Tibetans. The importance of the Tibetan plateau is colossal. It contains the Hindu Kush Himalaya Mountain Range, the origin of ten major river basins in Asia—Brahmaputra, Indus, Irrawaddy, Mekong, Salween, Sutlej, Yangtze, and Yellow Rivers. Known as the world's Third Pole, it forms the largest area of ice cover outside of the North and South Poles. Glaciers there are depleting faster than anywhere else on earth.[21] Nearly 1.9 billion people live in the ten river basins and more than three billion people are sustained by food produced in this area. This region is home to diverse cultures, languages, religions, and traditional knowledge systems. This region is undergoing rapid change driven by stressors such as climate change, human conflicts, infrastructure development, migration, urbanization, and tourism. The outcome of these complex drivers of change will have major global consequences.

I've heard the Dalai Lama say many times, earth is our only home and it is our interest to look after it, yet we not only don't take good care of it, we abuse it. He is imploring us to find ways of manufacturing that don't destroy our limited natural resources. He says we rely on technology to solve our problems when, the environment doesn't need to be fixed. The solution to environmental problems—global warming, pollution, depletion of resources, and other ecological disorders—rests with us. We need to change our behavior and exercise restraint.

INTERRELIGIOUS HARMONY

The Dalai Lama is the leading advocate of interreligious understanding and harmony and the prevention of conflicts based on religious differences. In one of the earliest talks he gave on Buddhist-Christian dialogue, at the Harvard Divinity School in 1979, he said his contact with the West confirmed his conviction that having one religion for the world is impossible and that we should not think our beliefs are superior to the beliefs of others.

The Dalai Lama says that many of the world's problems and conflicts emerge because we have lost sight of the basic humanity that binds us as a human family. He urges us not to put so much emphasis on how we differ but think of our commonality instead. To start with, we should see each other as fellow human beings. The Dalai Lama believes that it doesn't matter if a person is religious or not. What is more important is that they are good human beings. In fact, he says religion is a personal practice and should remain so. He explained how uncomfortable he was when asked to teach Buddhism to over 8,000 Buddhists in France.

I felt uncomfortable to teach Buddhism in a non-Buddhist country. If a non-Buddhist came to teach us we would feel uncomfortable. So, similarly in non-Buddhist countries, teaching Buddhism is not suitable. I was offered a lot of money to construct a Buddhist center in France. I told them this is not a Buddhist country, if you want to create a center either in Thailand or Sri Lanka or India it would be welcome. I told them to respect other religions. For individuals, it is ok, but creating a big institution, I don't like that.

On the surface, from a distant and superficial view, the Dalai Lama may appear to be the leader of a celebrity cult. He certainly has the charisma, and his laughter creates unites people and transcends cultures. When the Dalai Lama teaches in the West, he is careful about teaching Buddhism in non-Buddhist countries. He believes that different religions should not compete for followers and converts. He usually begins his teaching by saying something to the effect of, I don't want you non-Buddhists to be Buddhists. The Dalai Lama is not interested in gaining students nor is he interested in proselytizing Buddhism. He thinks it is not only impractical but wrong to do so as it is disrespectful of other religions. In fact, whenever there are large teachings where most people are not Buddhist, he tells them that it is best if people keep their original religion or adopt religious practices that are found in their own cultural background. His public talks for non-Buddhist audiences cover subjects such as peace, happiness, compassion, ethics, the environment, and social and gender issues. He has extracted the heart of Buddhist teachings and made them pragmatic and applicable in the modern world.

The Dalai Lama says, although there are many traditions in the world, each with a unique philosophy, fundamentally, they all teach the same message of love, compassion, forgiveness, tolerance, and self-discipline. All religions have the potential to create good human beings and help people lead meaningful and happy lives. The Dalai Lama wants the world's religions to respect and value each other instead of focusing on philosophical differences, which has led to fighting and bloodshed. Religious harmony is critical to building a peaceful and happy world. The Dalai Lama is the global champion of interreligious dialogue and has facilitated numerous interfaith talks. He has made inroads in developing understanding and tolerance between world religions.

The Dalai Lama distinguishes between individual practitioners and humanity. He feels individual practitioners must form their own truth based on their personal point of view. However, from a global perspective, there are many groups of individuals, each with many truths and many authentic paths.

> There is only one truth that is entirely valid and authentic for a given individual, from his or her own personal point of view. But from a global point of view, referring to a group of many individuals, we have to say that there are many truths and many authentic paths.

The Dalai Lama shows integrity. He is not leveraging religion; on the contrary, he is an advocate of universal ethics and says that if faith is a source of problems, as it has been throughout history and continues to be, then we should just have common sense. This is a unique and refreshing way of thinking outside-the-box. The Dalai Lama is willing to do what is right for the global world—even if it means promoting a secular approach. Buddhism is not an exception. He wants to be inclusive—he wants all seven billion humans to be happy and live a fulfilling life.

PEACE AND DISARMAMENT

The Dalai Lama has developed and promoted a model for nonviolence—active non-violence—which he has applied in his approach with China to resolve the Tibetan struggle. He has said that the Tibetan's opposition is towards Chinese policies and actions, not the people. He has made a distinction between the person and the action. Oppose the action, but remember the humanity of the person; challenge, question, oppose, and stand firm, but with a commitment to nonviolence. He often says that prayer is not enough—we need to act.

The Dalai Lama listens to BBC News every morning and has done so since his youth in Tibet. "Not a day goes by that somewhere in the world, something happens that everyone agrees is unfortunate." Those events which are caused by humans, "wars, crime, violence of every sort, corruption, poverty, deception, fraud, and social, political, and economic injustice are each the consequence of negative human behavior." He tells us emphatically, and I have seen him tap his chest to emphasize his point, "we are responsible for such behavior!" Fortunately, he reassures us, "these human problems, because they are all essentially ethical problems, can be overcome."

The Dalai Lama says through material development and progress, we have produced weapons of mass destruction which are capable of destroying a large populations of people. People consider these weapons to be important to their security and safety, so nations produce and use them. Using weapons to inflict harm on others has not solved human problems. Being motivated by attachment and hatred does not provide a foundation to resolve social problems. The Dalai Lama urges us to dialogue when there are disagreements. That's the only way, he explains. We need to make a commitment to strive towards a healthier humanity. Whenever we find disagreements, we must think, reason, and dialogue instead of going to war.

The Dalai Lama proposes the twenty-first century as a century of dialogue. He advocates for this: whenever we have a disagreement with someone, we ought to keep in mind their interest, our own interest, and our mutual interests, then find a mutually beneficial solution. Use reasoning, not combat, to demilitarize the world. It is his hope that this will be a century of peace, a century of dialogue—a century when a more caring, responsible, and compassionate humanity will emerge. He tells us to act out of concern for others. Provided we undertake that practice sincerely and persistently, "little by little, step by step we will gradually be able to reorder our habits and attitudes so that we think less about our own narrow concerns and more of others. In doing so, we will find that we enjoy peace and happiness for ourselves."[22]

VISION FOR TIBET: ZONE OF PEACE

The Dalai Lama continues to seek freedom for his people and the preservation of their livelihood and culture in Tibet. Despite the loss of a million Tibetans, the destruction of sacred institutions, monuments, and scriptures and the degradation and pollution of forests, pastures, and rivers, he continues to advocate nonviolence and dialogue as a solution. The Dalai Lama has consistently stated that the Tibetans are against the Chinese policy that has caused environmental destruction and atrocity but are not angry towards individual Chinese people.

The Tibetans consider Tibet to be an occupied land but are not seeking independence. Since 1974, Tibetans have campaigned for the same rights and privileges afforded to the Chinese people that are laid out in the Chinese constitution. The Middle Way Approach grew from this.

What the Tibetans proposed is this: the survival of Tibet's unique culture, and for the Chinese to give them meaningful autonomy so that Tibetans feel safe to practice their own culture and use their own language. This is a realistic approach to solving the problem. What it emphasizes is human value, human rights, and the protection of the environment. In 1987, the Dalai Lama outlined The Five Point Peace Plan to the U.S. Congress. In it, he called for the transformation of Tibet into a zone of peace, with respect for human rights, environmental protection, and the cessation of nuclear-waste disposal. The following year he addressed the European Parliament, where he presented a formal proposal for negotiations to serve as a basis for resolving the Tibet issue. The Central Government of the People's Republic of China would have responsibility for Tibet's international relations and defense while the Tibetan people would manage all affairs pertaining specifically to Tibet, such as religion, culture, education, economy, health, and ecological and environmental protection.

His Holiness' teaching of compassion has transformed the Tibet Freedom Movement from an aggressive movement into a non-violent one. The Middle Way Approach was proposed by the Dalai Lama as a peaceful resolution of the Tibet issue and was adopted democratically by Tibetans in exile in June 1988. Its aim is to bring about stability and co-existence between the Tibetan and Chinese peoples based on equality and cooperation. Tibetans seek autonomy, not independence, for all Tibetans living in the three provinces of Tibet within the People's Republic of China. This entity would have the status of national regional autonomy governed by a democratically elected legislature and executive, with an independent judicial system.

The Tibetans are not insisting on political separation of any kind. They want to be part of China, but they don't want mining in their fields. They want China's help in restoring areas of excessive deforestation and wildlife depletion. They want to restore the headwaters of all the rivers in India, China, Bangladesh, Myanmar, Nepal, Bhutan, and Southeast Asia that stem from Tibet. That would be in China's interest, too. If implemented, Tibet would be transformed into a zone of peace and non-violence. The proposed zone would have a Dharamsala-like atmosphere, attracting international tourists and spiritual seekers. It would be a zone of environmental peace under Chinese sovereignty.

The Middle Way has been the fundamental principle for dealings with the Chinese government. The Tibetans have repeatedly sought a mutually agreed upon solution to the ongoing Tibet freedom issue. The Chinese government views the Dalai Lama as their enemy and believes that his death will solve the problem. Although the Dalai Lama continues to be the voice for Tibetans and their aspiration for freedom, he has devolved his political authority to a democratically elected leadership. To this, the Dalai Lama has replied that the Tibet issue is not a Dalai Lama issue. After his death, the issue will continue to be carried out by the leadership of the Tibetan diaspora.

CONCLUSION

The Dalai Lama brings a viable alternative to a world weary of politicians and leaders who are not in tune with what is going on in the world; he brings new paradigms of positivity and hope. The Dalai Lama is a living model of the best qualities of a Buddhist monk: he is a fountain of wisdom; he strives to perfect himself and through this has become an example for others by his gentleness, wisdom, compassion, and good conduct. He is a giant among spiritual leaders and a model of genuine compassion, which can be experienced only when self-absorption is eliminated and replaced with the desire to help others. He is a true servant leader who aspires to serve all of humanity. True compassion brings internal serenity and peace which manifests as welcoming and understanding, all of which contributes to the promotion of peace and harmony. This is what we see when we meet the Dalai Lama, and through his eyes he makes us feel that we too can attain true compassion and can live as warm-hearted human beings in harmony with each other.

In addition to being a spiritual leader he has had years of experience as a leader of his people. In Tibet he witnessed the full fury of destructive forces thundering down on his land and his people and is still struggling to gain human rights and greater freedom for the Tibetan people in Tibet and the protection of Tibet's natural environment. Instead of engaging in violence, the Dalai Lama has engaged in peaceful nonviolent protest of the destruction of Tibetan culture and environment. He proposed Tibet to be designated as a nuclear free zone of peace where Tibetan people have the freedom to practice their culture, their human rights and democratic freedoms are respected, and Tibet's natural environment is restored and protected.

Despite the hardship he has encountered and the horrendous news he hears from his people in Tibet, he has, as we have witnessed, a sense of calmness derived from having inner peace of mind. There is sadness but not despair. With a calm and focused mind, he has rebuilt a modernized community in exile. Under his leadership, the Tibetan diaspora has made a transition from ancient hereditary rule to democratically elected leadership. Under his guidance, the Tibetans have been able to practice and preserve their culture. In doing so, they have shown us the importance of human values such as compassion and loving kindness.

The Dalai Lama invites all of us into his world, which he tells us, he shares with seven billion people. It is the same world we belong to but somehow it feels happier and safer and more inclusive and inviting to know that he is in the same world. Therefore, so many international visitors travel the long and winding road by bus or train to Dharamsala, believing they can simply drop in on the Dalai Lama. "We were traveling in India and came here for a day to meet His Holiness," they plead with the person responsible for handling such requests. Whenever possible, the visitors are granted a place in line the following morning.

During the New Year celebration I attended, so many people visited Dharamsala wanting to meet the Dalai Lama that he invited all international visitors to an impromptu gathering. Over 500 people from forty countries showed up. Instead of sitting inside his temple, he sat on a chair placed on the steps of the courtyard facing the visitors who sat on the courtyard floor. He wanted to emphasize that he was an equal among them. He first greeted the people with thanks for making the effort to come and visit him. Then, he spoke of some of his favorite themes: compassion—the ultimate source of a happy life is warmheartedness, interdependence—our interests and others' interests are very much interconnected because we are all part of the seven billion human beings and our survival totally depends on the care of others, altruism—if we think only of ourselves, even a tiny problem appears unbearable but if we think more about others' well-being our mind opens wider and our own problems appear insignificant. This was followed by a question-and-answer session. Even in this informal setting, he listened carefully to the questions and responded to them earnestly. If the questions raised points he perhaps hadn't previously considered, he would contemplate a bit longer. He was clearly enjoying exchanging ideas with people from many nations and of all ages and learning something new. It is his willingness to engage with and listen to everyone that makes others want to listen to him. It's part of how he gets his message across.

As the above example illustrates, access to the Dalai Lama is surprisingly easy, unlike situations surrounding other heads of state and religions. He gets visibly energized by greeting and meeting unexpected visitors. He is accessible and authentic: simply stated, what you see is what you get. He has nothing to hide, and his only agenda is to promote the development of the human potential.

Although the Dalai Lama is a devout and highly educated Buddhist, people from all faiths, as well as people without faith, reach out to him. The Dalai Lama touches us because he connects to our humanness. His message resonates with us because he speaks to our hearts as a fellow human being. He challenges us to see beyond our own national borders and our own lifetime and work towards a better future for everyone.

When the pandemic of 2020 spread globally, in response to requests from people around the world, the Dalai Lama took to the web to speak with all of us. He first showed his empathy but acknowledged that this is an exceptionally difficult time. Then he expressed his gratitude to governments across the world for taking steps to meet the challenges. To help encourage us, he reminded us that we have faced enormous challenges in the past and have shown a remarkable ability to survive. He then gave us an invaluable tool to help us stay calm.

> *Faced with threats to our health and well-being, it is natural to feel anxiety and fear. Nevertheless, I take great solace in the following wise advice to examine the problems before us: If there is something to be done—do it, without any need to worry; if there's nothing to be done, worrying about it further will not help.*

He speaks to us with the voice of optimism. His engagement is convincing because he speaks a very compelling truth.

The Dalai Lama has said that his power is his motivation, his sincerity, and his inner truth. His compassion, kindness, wisdom, and generosity towards us moves and inspires us. People around the world realize that everything in life has potential to be deeper and more meaningful. They seek fundamental change. For those seeking enduring happiness he has become a source of light. The actions that make him human, rather than a deity—walking, talking, and laughing—are ever present and often made me forget that he is the Dalai Lama. He is not an exceptional being or a deity, which many Tibetans believe him to be, but a great example of what a human being can be.

The Dalai Lama doesn't explicitly tell us what to do and how to live our lives. He says, when we listen to his teachings, we must critically examine what he says and take the part we agree with. At the end of my interview with the Dalai Lama, he said the same thing to me. He told me to tell the story I believe in. The Dalai Lama works in ways which make sense in hindsight. I understand why he gave me access to him. Had I relied on his interview, I would have missed observing how he guides and coaches people. I observed how he connects with everyone he meets. I also observed that people feel genuinely happy when they meet him. His love and kindness are inclusive—he accepts us as who we are. Unconditionally.

The Dalai Lama evokes powerful emotions from people. When people see my portrait of the Dalai Lama meditating, they burst into spontaneous smiles and say: "He exudes warmth and compassion. He makes me feel happy. He gives me great comfort. He is so peaceful." Are they responding to this photograph or has the photograph triggered innate feelings they have for the Dalai Lama? The Dalai Lama's message of peace and understanding and love and respect and his practice of kindness and compassion resonates with people globally, regardless of nationality, religion, race, culture, and all the identities that keep us apart. He truly believes that fundamentally, as human beings, we are all the same—we seek happiness and do not want suffering. He reminds us that we share a common humanity, and we have responsibility towards each other.

Reflecting to the pivotal day on the railroad platform in India, I see now that my life took an important turn. I spent over a decade traveling to places where the Tibetan diaspora live. I have been personally touched by their inner qualities of peace and compassion and wisdom. Then in 2018, I had the good fortune of meeting the Dalai Lama in person and was invited to photograph many of the traditional ceremonies and teachings he conducted as well as the Mind and Life Dialogue session. As I reflect on my meetings with the Dalai Lama, analyze his leadership, and contemplate why he is so successful, I understand why the Tibetans refer to him as *Kundun*, which means, the presence. He is a radiant power of goodness who believes that we too can achieve goodness. In the presence of Kundun, we too believe in ourselves and that we can make a difference in creating a kinder and more compassionate world. As a refugee from China, I feel a special connection with the Tibetan diaspora. The Dalai Lama has opened the gateway to include all humanity. He leads a compassionate life for a holistic world.

I close with the short prayer which the Dalai Lama says gives him inspiration in his quest to benefit others. This prayer reflects the wisdom and compassion of the Dalai Lama.[23]

May I become at all times, both now and forever
A protector for those without protection
A guide for those who have lost their way
A ship for those with oceans to cross
A bridge for those with rivers to cross
A sanctuary for those in danger
A lamp for those without lights
A place of refuge for those who lack shelter
And a servant to all in need

The Dalai Lama holding the mala beads he escaped Tibet with in his right hand.

BIBLIOGRAPHY

H.H. Dalai Lama, *My Land and My People*. New York: Warner Books, 1962.

_____, *The Dalai Lama: My Tibet*. University of California Press, 1989.

_____, *Freedom in Exile, The Autobiography of the Dalai Lama*. New York: Harper Collins, 1990.

_____, *The Good Heart*. London: Rider, 1997.

_____, *Ethics for the New Millennium*. New York: Riverhead Books, 1999.

_____ *The Universe in a Single Atom: The Convergence of Science and Spirituality*. New York: Morgan Road Books, 2005.

_____, *Beyond Religion: Ethics for a Whole World*. New York: Rider, an imprint of Ebury Publishing, 2012

_____, *Science and Philosophy in the Indian Buddhist Classics. Vol. 1: The Physical World*. New York: Simon and Schuster, 2018 (Editor Thupten Jinpa)

_____Collected Statements and Articles. Dharamsala: DIIR Publications, 1986.

Harrington, Anne and Zajonc, Arthur, ed. *The Dalai Lama at MIT*. First Harvard University Press, 2008.

Hindu Kush Himalaya Assessment Report, 2019. (online)

The Dalai Lama Global Vision Summit, presented by Lion's Roar and Tibet House, USA. October 22–27, 2020

Dali Lama's public talks on zoom

ACKNOWLEDGMENTS

I began this project under the guidance of Rinchen Dharlo, president of The Tibet Fund. He has subsequently retired from the role after thirty years at the helm. His many years of working for the Tibetan government in exile in India, Nepal, and North American enabled him to generate a comprehensive itinerary and invaluable contact list for me, which highlighted all the key people and places to photograph. As a highly respected leader in the Tibetan community, his personal introduction granted remarkable access to people doing important work for the Tibetan community in exile in all areas—education, cultural preservation, social services, and exile government. I am extremely grateful for his kindness and wisdom.

The late Dorje Gyaltsen, from the Home Office in Dharamsala, accompanied me and acted as a translator and an interpreter of Tibetan language and culture in my early travels. In my later trips to southern India and Nepal, when he couldn't accompany me, he contacted the people I was to meet daily to remind them of my upcoming visit. Rinchen Dharlo said this project wouldn't have gone so smoothly without Dorje's dedication.

In 2018, I had the good fortune of meeting the Dalai Lama who gave me, as Chhime R. Chhoekyapa, Secretary, Office of HH the Dalia Lama said, unprecedented access. In my journey to make this book possible, I want to share my gratitude to all the Tibetans I met along the way who shared their warmth and generosity with me. I also want to acknowledge the people who helped shape my project after my travels—readers, writing coaches, and mentors, for whom the unifying factor was a love of Tibet and its people. It was wonderful sharing this unique life experiences with them.

I want to thank all the people for all their support with special thanks to all those individuals and organizations listed on the following pages.

PEOPLE INTERVIEWED AND CONSULTED

Chetsang Rinpoche, 37th throne holder

Delek Yangdon, Dolma Ling Nunnery

Dhondup Dorje, Settlement Officer, Rawangla

Diki Tsering, Executive Director, Diki DayCare Center, New York

Dorje Gyaltsen, Project Officer, Department of Home

Geshe Dawa, Drikung Kagyu Lineage

Geshe Namgyal, Abbot of Namgyal Monastery

Gyalo Thondup, Former Kalon Tripa Prime Minister of CTA

Hermits, Dharamsala

Jamma Dhondrup, Chief Tibetan Officer, Nepal

Jampa Nobling

Jampa Phuntso, Settlement Officer, Rabgayling

Jampa Phuntsok, Principal, Srongtsen School, Nepal

Jampal Kalden, Local Assembly, Kalimpong

Jetsun Cheme, President, Tibetan Women's Association, New York

Jetsun Pema, President of the Tibetan Children's Village for 42 years

Jigme Jungney, Member of Parliament

Jingir-Pon Damdul, Settlement Officer, Lugsung Samdupling

Karma Singay, Settlement Officer, Kollegal

Kalsang and Dolker Dorje, USA

Kelsang Phuntsok Jungney, Tibetan Association of Northern California (TANC)

Khenpo Karten Rinpoche, Manjushuri Dharma Center, USA

Khube Rinpoche, Karuna Handicap Center

Kunga Dorje, Chief Representative, Bangalore, Department of Home

Kunga Tashi - Office of Tibet, USA

Ling Rinpoche

Lhakdor, Director, Library of Tibetan Works and Archives

Lobsang Gyatso

Lobsang Nyandak, The Tibet Fund

Matthieu Ricard, Shechen Monastery, Nepal

Namgyal Lhamo Taklha, Former CTA Secretary, Dehradun

Ngawang Dorje, Director, SOS Children's Village

Ngodup Dorje, Secretary, Department of Home

Palden Dhondup, Settlement Officer, Doeguling

Pat Upson, United Kingdom

Pema Dorje Tibetan Language Class, New York

Penpa Tsering - Office of Tibet. Currently Sikyong of the Central Tibetan Administration

Rinchen Khando Choegyal, Tibetan Nuns Project, President of Women's

Tibetan Association,
Rinzin Wangmo, Secretary, Doeguling Settlement
Robert Thurman, Buddhist author and academic, USA
Samdhong Lobsang Tenzin Rinpoche, Kalon Tripa, Prime Minister of CTA (2001-2011)
Serta Tsulrim Woeser, Member of Parliament
Sonam Choephel, Secretary, Kollegal Settlement
Sonam Gyatso, President, Tibetan Community of New York and New Jersey (TCNYNJ)
Sonam Paldon
Susan Bauer-Wu, President of the Mind and Life Institute
Tashi Dolma, USA, nomad dentist
Tashi Lhamo, Project Manager, Dikey Larso Settlement
Tashi Phuntsok, Member of Parliament
Tashi Tsering Phuri, Director, Men-Tsee-Khang (Tibetan Medical and Astro Institute)
Tenzin Choephel Chumeegal, the Tibet Fund
Tenzin Nobling, Settlement Officer, Darjeeling
Tenzin Sangmo, nomad in Ladakh
Tenzin Geyche Tethong, former Secretary, Office of HH the Dalai Lama

Tenzin Nobling, Settlement Officer, Darjeeling
Tenzin Tethong Namgyal, former Kalong Tripa of CTA
Thinley Gyatso, Chief Tibetan officer, Kathmandu
Thupten Lungrik, Education Minister, CTA
Thupten Chakrishar, Himalayan Elders, USA
Thupten Ngodup, Tibet's Chief State Oracle
Thupten Sherab. Himalayan Elder, USA
Tsering Topgyal, Snow Lion Foundation, Nepal
Tashi Phuntsok, Member of Parliament
Tseten Kunsang
Tsewang Namgyal
Yangzom Shawa, the Tibet Fund
Yeshi Choedon, Settlement Officer, Hunsur

OFFICE OF HIS HOLINESS THE DALAI LAMA IN DHARAMSALA

His Holiness, the Dalai Lama
Chhime R. Chhoekyapa, Secretary
Ngawang Sonam - interpreter, Dharamsala
Tenzin Taklha, Additional Secretary
Tseten Samdup Chhoekyapa, Additional Secretary
Tenzin Jamphel, photographer

Thank you to the following people for their invaluable feedback on my manuscript and photography.

READERS

Bonnie Bollwinkel
Gillian Laidlaw
Sunny Lemoine
Lisa Okubo
Jeffrey M. Shaw

VISUAL CONSULTANTS

Eleni Antonopoulou
Elizabeth Avedon
Kevin Bransfield
Lucia Chih
William Giles
Carol Henry
Ann Jastrab
Robin V. Robinson
Ryuijie
Barbara Bullock Wilson
Jonathan Wolf

PLACES VISITED

SETTLEMENTS AND TIBETAN COMMUNITIES IN INDIA

Bir Tibetan Settlements (Dege, Nangchen Chauntr, Tibetan Society)
Darjeeling
Dekyiling Settlement, Dehradun
Dharamsala
Doeguling Tibetan Settlement, Mundgod
Dhondenling Tibetan Settlement, Kollegal
Dhondupling, Clementown, Dehradun
Dikyi Larso Tibetan Settlement, Bylakupee
Gangtok, Sikkim
Kalimpong
Kunphenling Tibetan Settlement, Ravangla, Sikkim
Lingtsang, Munduwala
Lugsung Samdupling Settlement, Bylakuppe
Rabgyeling Tibetan Settlement, Hunsur
Samyeling, Delhi
Sonamling Tibetan Settlement, Ladakh
Tashiling, Sonada
Tibetan Bonpo Foundation, Dolanji

SETTLEMENTS AND TIBETAN COMMUNITIES IN NEPAL

Jampaling Settlement, Lodrik, Helitar
Paljorling Settlement, Lodrik, Pokhara
Samdupling Settlement, Jawalakhel, Kathmandu
Tashi Palkhiel Settlement, Pokhara
Tashiling Settlement, Pokhara

TIBETAN COMMUNITIES VISITED IN THE WEST

Tibetan Association of Santa Fe, New Mexico
Tibetan Association of Northern California (TANC), Richmond, California
Tibetan Community of New York and New Jersey (TCNYNJ), Elmhurst, New York
Tibet Institute, Rikon, Switzerland

MONASTERIES, NUNNERIES, TEMPLES

Dolma Ling Nunnery and Institute, Kangra Valley near Dharamsala
Drepung Deyang Monastery, Mundgod
Drepung Loseling Monastery, Mundgod
Drukpa Kagyu Monastery, Bir
Drikung Kagyu Samtenling Nunnery, Dehradun
Drikung Kagyu Monastery, Dehradun
Dzogchen Monastery, Kollegal
Dzongsar Monastery, Chauntra
Ganden Namgyeling Monastery, Mundgod
Gyumed Tantric University, Hunsur
Gyuto Monastery, Dharamsala
Jamyang Choling Institute and Nunnery, Gharoh
Jangchub Choeling Nunnery, Mundgod
Kopan Monastery, Kathmandu, Nepal
Keydong Thuk Che Cho Ling Nunnery, Kathmandu, Nepal
Lamayuru Monastery, Ladakh
Mindrolling Monastery, Chementown, Dehradun
Namdroling Monastery, Bylakuppe
Namgyal Monastery, Dharamsala
Nechung Dorje Drayang Ling Monastery, Dharamsala
Phyang Monastery, Ladakh
Sakya Monastery, Dehradun
Sera Jey Monastery, Bylakuppe
Sera Mey Monastery, Bylakuppe
Shartse Monastery, Mundgod

Shechen Monastery, Kathmandu
Tana Monastery, Kollegal
Tashi Lhunpo Monastery, Bylakuppe
Tharpa Choling Monastery, Kalimpong
Tibetan Buddhist Dialectic Institution, Dharamsala
Tsuglagkhang Temple, Dharamsala
Yungdrung Bon Monastic Centre, Dolanji

INSTITUTIONS AND CENTERS IN INDIA

Delek Hospital, Dharamsala
Institute of Performing Tibetan Arts, Dharamsala
Institute of Small Trade Learning Center, Neela Mangala, near Bangalore
Jampaling Edler's Home, Dharamsala
Karuna Home for the Disabled, Bylakupee
Library for Tibetan Works and Archives, Dharamsala
Men-Tsee-Khang, Tibetan Medical and Astrological Institute, Dharamsala
Norbulingka Institute, near Dharamsala
Office of Information of the Tibetan Government in Exile
Srongtsen Library, Dehradun
Tibetan Refugee Reception Centre, Dharamsala
Tibetan Self Help Center, Darjeeling
Tibetan Women's Handicraft Centre, Dharamsala

SCHOOLS IN INDIA AND NEPAL

Central School for Tibetans, Mussoorie
Model School, Gamroo, Dharamsala
Ngoenga School for Tibetan Children with special needs
Srongtsen Bhrikuti High School, Boudha, Kathmandu, Nepal
Tibetan Children's Village (TCV) - throughout India
Tibetan School, Gangtok
Tibetan SOS Vocational Training Centre
Transit School, Dharamsala

ENDNOTES

1   *The Dalai Lama, My Land and My People: The Original Autobiography of His Holiness the Dalai Lama of Tibet.* New York: Grand Central Publishing, 1997.

2   Inspiration From Afar: How Tibet Informs the Dalai Lama's Value and Teachings, Thupten Jinpa. October 26, 2020. Transcript from The Dalai Lama Global Vision Summit, Lion's Roar and Tibet House US, October 22-27, 2020.

3   *The Dalai Lama, Freedom in Exile, The Autobiography of the Dalai Lama.* New York: Harper Collins, 1990. Page 80-81.

4   *The Dalai Lama, My Tibet,* 1989, p. 79.

5   Ven. Delek Yangdon. Interview. By Ginger Chih. 2018

6   Rinchen Khandro Choegyal. Interview. By Ginger Chih. 2018

7   The Dalai Lama, Public Talk, Nagajurna's Commentary on Bodhicitta, January 14-16, 2018.

8   The Dalai Lama, Ethics for the New Millennium, page 22-13.

9   The Dalai Lama, Ethics, page 26.

10   The Dalai Lama, Ethics, page 146.

11   The Dalai Lama, Ethics, page 162.

12   The Dalai Lama, Ethics, page 170.

13   The Dalai Lama, Ethics, page 237.

14   The Dalai Lama, Ethics, page,174.

15   The Universe in a Single Atom: The Convergence of Science and Spirituality, p. 30.

16   The Dalai Lama, Global Vision Summit, R. Davidson, Day 4 talk.

17   The Dalai Lama, MIT, p. 10-11

18   The Dalai Lama, The Universe in a Single Atom, p. 206.

19   The Dalai Lama, The Universe in a Single Atom, p. 208.

20   The Dalai Lama, Ethics, p. 189

21   Hindu Kush Himalaya Assessment Report, 2019

22   The Dalai Lama, Ethics, p. 236

23   The Dalai Lama, Ethics, p. 237